ACT NOW

Six Award Winning One Act Plays

By
Eileen Enwright Hodgetts

PERFORMANCE RIGHTS

The plays contained in this book are protected by copyright and all performance rights remain with the author.

The author gives permission for the plays herein to be performed royalty free by schools, colleges, and community theatre groups.

This work may not be photocopied, or reproduced in any way, including electronic reproduction. Permission for performance is given only if sufficient copies of the script are purchased for the proposed production, one for each performer, one for the director, and one for the stage manager.

Professional groups may apply for permission to produce subject to payment of royalties.

Scripts may be used for classroom work, or table-reads, but the author requires advance notice of any intended public performance.

The author may be contacted by e-mail at encounteru@comcast.net

Published by Emerge Publishing

INDEX

VISITORS
An Appalachian One Act
Finalist Pittsburgh New Works Festival

A battered wife refuses to leave her husband and her trailer court home because she is expecting visitors from "out there". A story of hope in hard circumstances

3 W

Nanc: A comfortable middle-aged woman
Holly: Young and feisty
Lena: A battered wife with a secret

Exterior scene, a trailer park in a poor rural area of the United States. We are outside Lena's trailer. Rickety steps go up to the front door. The front yard is littered with items that won't fit into the trailer. There are a couple of broken down lawn chairs, a battered picnic table and a clothes line, and some dense foliage by the front door. Holly and Nance: are hesitating at the foot of the steps. Holly is a young woman, in cutoff jeans, and a tight tee shirt. Nance is older, in stretch pants and a baggy tee shirt. It is nighttime, August. We have a sense that the day has been unbearably hot, and the night won't be much cooler.

NANCE : Are you sure they're gone?
HOLLY: Yeah, I seen them leaving. Their lights was flashing when they went past my place. Kenny was looking out the window, you know, asking me what the police was doing here?
NANCE: They're here most nights.

HOLLY: But not right next door. I mean, not at Lena's place.

NANCE: You ain't been here long, honey, so you don't understand. They always at Lena's place. Every six months or so old Joe Bob goes out of his skull and Lena, she calls the police.

HOLLY: She don't need the police, she needs a good lawyer.

NANCE: Yeah, well, she don't know no lawyers.

HOLLY: My boyfriend Spike's got a good lawyer, kept him out of jail a couple of times.

NANCE: Ain't there never gonna be no decent people moving in here?

HOLLY: I'm decent. I mind my own business. My kids are clean. They don't go running in and out of people's trailers making trouble, not like some I could mention.

NANCE: Okay, Okay, I didn't mean you. You're a good enough neighbor and I ain't never seen your boyfriend doing nothing.

HOLLY: He don't; not no more. So you reckon we should knock, if the police are gone and all?

NANCE: No. I reckon we should mind our own business. I been minding my own business here for more'n twenty years and I ain't never got into no trouble from minding my own business. If people gotta live all cooped up together like this, they gotta mind their own business.

HOLLY: Yeah, but we're, like, neighbors. I mean, we should see if she's all right, shouldn't we? She was screaming pretty good before the police came.

NANCE: If she needed hospital, they'd have taken her. All they took was him.

7

HOLLY: Yeah, well, good riddance to him. She's better off without him.

NANCE: Maybe she don't want to be on her own.

HOLLY: Better than being with him.

NANCE: Yeah well, I guess you never been on your own.

HOLLY: No, I ain't. I mean, there was my Mom, and my brothers, and then my boys and...

NANCE: So you don't know what you're talking about.

HOLLY: I only meant that...

NANCE: He's coming back you know.

HOLLY: Who?

NANCE: My husband.

HOLLY: I wasn't talking 'bout your husband. I don't know nothing about your husband.

NANCE: He's coming back.

HOLLY: Most of 'em don't.

NANCE: You some kind of expert or something?

HOLLY: No.

NANCE: Then mind your own business and don't go making remarks about things you don't understand.

HOLLY: I'm sorry; it just that it makes me mad, you know, a man like that beating up on a little old woman like Lena.

NANCE: She ain't all that old. We was in High School together.

HOLLY: She looks old.

NANCE: Well, it's hard for her, living with Joe Bob and all. Well, are you gonna knock, or are we gonna stand out here all night? I'm missing Duck Dynasty..

HOLLY: It's a re-run. They're all re-runs this time of year.

Okay, I'll knock. *She climbs the steps and hesitates with her hand on the door.* Maybe you should knock. I mean, she knows you, and she don't really know me.

NANCE: Okay, okay, if we're gonna do it, then let's get on with it. *She climbs the steps and knocks firmly on the door. No Answer.*

Lena, honey, it's Nance. Are you all right in there?
No answer.

HOLLY: Maybe she's got a concussion. He was beating her pretty good. Maybe she's got, like, delayed concussion.

NANCE: *Knocking harder.* Lena, honey, open the door.

HOLLY: Are you all right, Miss Lena? *(To Nance)* You reckon we should call the police to come back and check on her?

NANCE: Twice in one night? You'll be giving this place a bad name. Come on Lena, open the door. It's just me and Holly from next door. We just wanna know if you're all right.

The door opens slowly and Lena comes timidly into the light. She's a small woman, who carries herself with an air of defeat. She has a bruised face and is clasping one arm as though it hurts her.

LENA: Hello Nance.

NANCE: Hello, dear.

HOLLY: Are you all right, Miss Lena? We saw, you know, what happened.

LENA: Yeah, I guess everybody saw.

NANCE: You all right, honey?

LENA: I'm okay. They took him away.

NANCE: Yes, I know.

LENA: They're gonna call me and tell me how he's doing.

HOLLY: Do you care how he's doing?

NANCE: He's her husband.

HOLLY: But he beats her.

LENA: Not all the time. He don't beat me all the time.

HOLLY: Once is enough. If Spike laid so much as one finger on me, I'd throw his sorry ass out of my place as fast as you could say...

LENA: I can't do that. This is his place, you know.

HOLLY: You're his wife, ain't you? It's your place too. You can kick him out.

NANCE: I don't think Lena wants to talk about this right now. Here, honey, come and sit down. Don't go back into that stuffy old trailer. It's cool out here. You'll feel better.

LENA: I gotta be able to hear the phone. They gonna call me, you know.

NANCE Yeah, I know.

HOLLY: So you just gonna let him get away with it?

NANCE: Holly, mind your own business. Lena and Joe Bob been man and wife for thirty years. It ain't up to us to tell her what to do.

HOLLY: Well, I know what I'd do. Come on, Miss Lena. It's time to stand up for yourself. They'll charge him you know, and he'll get, like treatment, and all. You gotta do something? You can't let him go on like that.

LENA: I already done it.

NANCE: Done what?

LENA: *(Mysteriously)* Something.

NANCE: What you done, honey? You gonna get him charged?

LENA: Nope. But I done something. I done it years ago, and one day, one day....

*Her voice trails off and she moves away, looking up at the night sky.*Yeah, one day.

HOLLY: What you done, Miss Lena?

LENA: It's a secret. *(She turns, suddenly animated)* But I don't want you thinking I'm some stupid little old woman who just puts up with shit from her man 'cause she don't know no better. I know better, but I know something that none of y'ouns know. Yeah, I got a secret. *(She points up at the night sky.)* I got a secret out there.

(Moving her arm has obviously caused her pain and she grimaces as she brings it down again.)

NANCE: You should get that arm looked at.

LENA: I don't want no doctors looking at me. I don't never let no doctors to look at me. I don't want them to find "it".

NANCE: Find what?

LENA: Never you mind.

HOLLY: Let me look, Miss Lena. I know a bit about breaks and sprains and things. I got me two boys, I gotta know about stuff like that.

LENA: Okay, you can look. But only my arm. Don't go looking at nothing else.

HOLLY: Here, sit down. *She starts to look at Lena's arm.*

NANCE: What's this secret you talking about, Lena? I've knowed you all my life. You ain't got no secrets.

LENA: You don't know everything 'bout me. No one

11

knows everything 'bout me.

*Holly starts to look at Lena's bruised eye, but Lena pulls away.*No, don't go messing with that. There ain't no need for you to be looking at my face. How's my arm?

HOLLY: I don't think it's broken.

LENA: *(Laughing harshly)* It'll take more than Joe Bob Williams to break me. I bend, but I don't break.

HOLLY: Why do you let him do it to you?

LENA: 'Cause I can't stop him.

HOLLY: You could leave. Go to a battered woman's shelter or something. My sister done that and they was real good to her.

LENA: *(Vehemently)* I can't leave here. I can't never leave here. I have to be here when...when...

NANCE: When what, honey?

LENA: Never you mind. I can't leave, that's all.

NANCE: Okay, honey. Don't get yourself upset. You don't have to leave.

LENA: I can't be away. Not even one night. I might miss them, you know.

HOLLY: Miss who?

LENA: Nothing. Nothing at all. I'm saying too much.

NANCE: You're just upset about Joe Bob.

LENA: *Looking out at the night sky again.* Sometimes I want to tell him. I just want to scream it into his stupid ass face. I got friends, I wanna say. I got friends and one day they're gonna come, and they're gonna mess you up so good, and they're gonna take me and... and....

NANCE: Lena, honey, what on earth are you talking about?

LENA: Nothing. Nothing. I just wish they'd come, that's all. Tonight'd be a good night. Yeah, night like this, that's when they come, you know. Nights like this.

NANCE: When who come?

LENA: *Gesturing vaguely at the stars* Them.

HOLLY: You mean angels, Miss Lena? You looking for angels to come?

LENA: No, not angels. I ain't looking for no angels. I don't believe in no angels.

HOLLY: You should you know. My sister's got this angel book, and it says angels can do all sorts of things for you. Stuff you can't do for yourself. I got china angels, you know, for my boys, put 'em up high so they won't break 'em.

NANCE: You talking about friends, Lena? You got some friends somewhere that are gonna come and get you, is that it?

LENA: No. Not friends. No. *She rises and walks downstage again.* How long have I gotta wait? that's what I want to know. I been patient, you know, but sometimes I wonder if they're ever coming. What if they don't come, Nance? What if they never come?

NANCE: Who, honey? Who you talking about?

LENA: *Pointing at the stars again.* Them.

HOLLY: *Following the direction of her pointing finger.* Up there? People from up there?

LENA: *(Defiantly)* Yeah.

HOLLY: Angels?

LENA: No.

13

NANCE: People from up there?

LENA: Yeah.

NANCE: Up in the sky?

LENA: No, not the sky.

NANCE: Space? People from space?

LENA: *(Still defiant)* Yes.

NANCE: You're waiting for space people?

HOLLY: You mean like little green men from Mars? *(To Nance)* She wouldn't let me look at her head, but she's got bruises, you know. He's been beating her around the head.

LENA: It ain't nothing to do with Joe Bob. I ain't making this up. I seen them. Years ago, I seen them.

NANCE: Honey, I don't think you know what you're saying.

LENA: Sure I know. I know just what I'm saying. I saying I seen men and they wasn't from here. They came down out of the sky, on a night like this. Just like this. Right here. Right in this trailer park. And I seen them.

NANCE: Well, how come you never said anything? When was this?

LENA: 1991.

NANCE: I was living here in 1991, and I didn't see no men from Mars. Nobody here seen no men from Mars.

LENA: I seen them. They come down right over there.

HOLLY: Was you drinking, Miss Lena? I heard you used to be a drinker.

LENA: See, that's why I ain't never told nobody. I knew they'd laugh. I knew there wouldn't be no one believe me.

I wouldn't tell you now, 'cept I don't like the way that girl there's looking at me.

HOLLY: Me? What's the matter with the way I'm looking at you?

LENA: Like I'm some old fool woman without sense enough to get while the going's good. Yeah, I hear what you saying about shelters and court cases and all that other stuff, but, see, if I do that, then I won't be here when they comes, and I gotta be here when they comes. I know what you're thinking, missie, but I ain't no fool. I got a plan. I got a way out of here, so don't you go looking at me all pitying like. I don't need no pity. I don't need no one's pity.

NANCE: Lena, look at me. Now you just stop all this wild talk and tell me what you really talking 'bout.

LENA: I'm talking about August 24, 1991, and you wasn't here that night.

NANCE: August 24, that's the night my Larry was born.

LENA: And you wasn't here. And Joe Bob he weren't here neither. He was working nights then down at Millers Truck Stop.

NANCE: Okay, okay, so you was on your own. So what happened?

LENA: I was awake, you know, 'cause I heard you leaving to go to the hospital. I reckon all the door slamming and hollering woke me up. So I'm lying there, and the moon's shining in my window and I'm thinking about you and wondering how it would be to going to the hospital for a baby. *(To Holly)* I never had no babies.

HOLLY: I'm sorry.

LENA: You don't have to be sorry. It don't matter to me no more. So I guess I goes back to sleep and then I wake up again 'cause there's this smell.

HOLLY: Was it a kinda sweet smell?

LENA: Well no...

HOLLY: That's angels. I heard about that. See what with the baby being born and all, I bet there was angels around. They say there's a real sweet smell with angels.

LENA: It was a stink. A real rotten stink.

HOLLY: Demons. You seen demons. Oh sweet heaven, there been demons here. No wonder there's so much trouble here, Miss Lena's husband beating her up, and Miss NANCE:'s husband running off like that. Oh, I gotta go. I can't let my boys be getting into trouble. If there's demons here I...

NANCE: Holly Mitchells will you just shut up about angels and demons. Let this woman tell her story and close that stupid mouth of yours.

HOLLY: But I...

NANCE: Shut up.

HOLLY: Huh.

NANCE: *(To Lena)* So what happened then?

LENA: Well, I start, you know, wondering where this smell is coming from, and I gets up to see if it's like inside the trailer, or outside. Well, it ain't inside, so I comes out, down those steps, and it was real quiet out here. *She walks downstage again.* The night was kinda bright, but no moon, no stars, just bright. Wasn't like it is now with lights from all them houses and such. There weren't much here then, just a few trailers and no lights, but it was bright, and there was a wind blowing, hot, sticky, worse than the daytime. It was strange, real strange.

HOLLY: What about the smell?

LENA: I don't know. I came down here to the fence. I remember putting my hand on the fence, and I remember something about my hair.

NANCE Your hair?

LENA: It was hurting. Like someone was pulling it.

HOLLY: And then what?

LENA: I don't know. I didn't know nothing until morning. I was in my own bed and it was morning.

HOLLY: That don't sound like demons.

NANCE: Shut up about the demons.

HOLLY: I don't get what the big secret's all about. A bad smell and someone pulling her hair; that ain't no big secret.

LENA: No. *(She puts her hand up into her hair behind her ear and pulls out a small, metal object.)* This is the big secret.

HOLLY: What is it?

LENA: Something they give me.

HOLLY: Let me see it.

LENA: No.

HOLLY: If you want me to believe you, you gotta let me see it.

LENA: *Handing it over reluctantly* All right, but you be real careful. I don't want nothing to happen to it.

17

NANCE: Where'd you find that thing, Lena?

LENA: In my hair. I found it when I woke up. I reckon they put it there. I reckon that's why I felt like someone was pulling my hair. That was them, putting it in there.

NANCE: So what do you think it is?

LENA: It's so as they can talk to me. So they can tell me when they coming back.

NANCE: You reckon?

LENA: Yeah. They coming back to get me.

NANCE: But if you don't remember nothing 'bout them...

LENA: I remember some.

NANCE: More than just the hair pulling and the smell?

LENA: Way more. But I didn't remember it all at once, like. It's come to me slowly in little pieces. Sometimes at night I get little, you know, flashes. I'll be sleeping and then suddenly like, I'll remember something. One night I woke up and my arm, this one *(indicating her injured arm)* had gone to sleep, and it was kinda, you know, tingling, and then I remembered them doing something to my arm. I remember them holding it, and they had thin hands, very warm, very gentle. They was holding my arm, stroking it, I think.

NANCE: They didn't hurt you, then?

LENA: No. They're my friends. They don't hurt me. I think they did something else; something kinda... you gonna think I'm real stupid saying this, Nance.

NANCE: No, go ahead, say it.

LENA: *Looking at Holly out of the corner of her eye, but Holly is absorbed in examining the metal device.* Come over

18

here, I don't want her to hear me, she won't understand.

NANCE: She's not listening. What is it? What do you think they did?

LENA: Well, you know.

NANCE: No, Lena, I don't know.

LENA: Something... Something...

NANCE: You mean, like sex?

LENA: Shh. Yeah, something like that. Kinda made me warm all over, made me feel real good.

NANCE: You remember that?

LENA: Not then. But I remember it now.

NANCE: Why would they do that?

LENA: Well, I been thinking 'bout that, and I been thinking it wasn't well, like romantic or nothing. I mean, I don't suppose I looked real good to them, them being thin and kinda blue, and me being, well, you know, human. So I don't reckon it was anything like that. I reckon it was a breeding thing.

NANCE: Lena, what are you saying?

LENA: I reckon they was getting me pregnant.

NANCE: But you ain't had no babies.

LENA: Not yet.

NANCE: You mean, you think that all this time....?

LENA: Yeah, why not? I mean, who knows how long it might take to make one of their babies.

NANCE: But wouldn't you know? Wouldn't you feel it?

LENA: Not if it weren't in the normal place. I mean, I been thinking. Maybe that was what they was doing to my arm. *(Becoming highly excited)* Or it could be in my head, it might come out of my ear, or my eyeball, or my big toe or my...

HOLLY: Hey, what's the matter with her?

NANCE: Don't ask.

LENA: See, I knew this would happen. That's why I didn't never tell no one. You don't believe me. I know you don't.

NANCE: Well, honey, it is kinda hard.

LENA: All right then, so you don't believe me. So tell me something, huh? If I'm making this all up. If I didn't see nothing, and if I don't have no alien probe in my brain, and no alien baby in my arm...

HOLLY: What did she say?

NANCE: You don't wanna know.

LENA: If I don't have none of them things, then what am I doing here? How come I didn't leave years ago? I coulda gone somewhere else years ago, and I coulda found me another man, but I stayed here. And you know why I did that? I did that so as I could come out here on nights like this, and I could look up at the stars and I could think about them coming to get me. Leaving that star of theirs way out there and coming all the way back here; and I have to be here. They coming all the way across sky, that's a long way to come, I gotta be patient and wait for them, and I can't let no stupid little Joe Bob Williams get in their way. But when they come... when they come...

She is interrupted by the telephone ringing in the trailer.

HOLLY: Your phone's ringing.

LENA: I know that. I ain't deaf. It'll be the police. They gonna ask me about charges.

HOLLY: You gonna charge him?

LENA: Ain't you listened to a word I said? I can't be going down there, I gotta wait here. No, I ain't gonna charge him.

She goes up the steps and into the trailer. The phone stops ringing.

HOLLY: She has a baby in her arm?

NANCE: Maybe.

HOLLY: Don't tell me you believe her?

NANCE: No, of course not. So, did you look at it? What is it?

HOLLY: Some piece of shit, made in China.

NANCE: You sure?

HOLLY: *Holding it out in the palm of her hand* It looks like a watch battery.

NANCE: Yeah, sure does, but you can't be sure, you know. I mean, it don't say watch battery on it.

HOLLY: It don't say "alien mind probe" neither.

NANCE: Made in China, you sure?

HOLLY: Somewhere lIke that. It sure ain't made in the US of A.

NANCE: But it says "made in China"?

HOLLY: No, but it's covered all over in Chinese writing.

NANCE: You sure it's Chinese?

HOLLY: Chinese, Japanese, some Oriental shit like that. It ain't nothing. The woman's crazy.

Pause

NANCE: You read Chinese?

HOLLY: No.

NANCE: So we don't know it's Chinese.

HOLLY: Look at it for yourself.

She tosses it to Nance but it falls into the bushes by the steps.

HOLLY: Shit.

NANCE: What you go and do that for?

They start peering into the bushes.

HOLLY: Damn it's dark in there. We ain't never gonna find it. It's just a little bitty thing.

NANCE: We gotta find it.

HOLLY: Yeah, well, I'm doing my best.

NANCE: Why d'ya have to go and throw it? I ain't never been much of a one for catching.

HOLLY: *Straightening up* I can't see nothing in there.

Lena enters from the trailer.

LENA: They're gonna keep him all... what you doing in my bushes?

HOLLY: Nothing. What was you saying Miss Lena?

LENA: I said they gonna keep him all night. Gonna send him home in the morning when he's sobered up.

HOLLY: And you ain't gonna charge him.

LENA: No, I ain't, I already told you that.

NANCE: You should go to bed. Get a good night's sleep while you can.

LENA: No. I'm just gonna sit out here and look at the sky.

HOLLY: No, really, you should go to bed. I mean you been beat up pretty bad.

LENA: I'll go to bed tomorrow. Joe Bob'll be quiet as a lamb when he comes home. He's always quiet for a couple of days after... after... well, you know.

NANCE: But you look tired.

LENA: What are you two playing at? Why you trying to get me to go to bed?

HOLLY: It's kinda late, Miss Lena.

LENA: Then you go to bed. Where's my communicator?

HOLLY: Your what?

LENA: You know what I'm talking about. My communicator. The thing I gave you to look at. Give it back.

HOLLY: Yeah, well, I...

LENA: Give it back.

HOLLY: I ain't got it, Miss Lena.

LENA: *(To Nance:)* Give it back to me.

NANCE: We dropped it.

LENA: Dropped it? What d'ya mean. I just gave it to you to hold for a moment. How did you drop it? Is it broke?

NANCE: No. Leastways, I don't think so. It fell into the bushes.

HOLLY: But we can't see it. Maybe it rolled under your trailer.

LENA: *Flying at her furiously.*   Find it. You gotta find it. Don't you understand nothing. Where is it? Which bush. Come on, help me.

HOLLY: We can find it in the morning.

LENA: No, no. What if they come tonight? We gotta find it.
Lena starts to search feverishly through the bushes

NANCE: Don't do that, honey. You just making it worse. Look you're trampling on everything. You gotta do this slow and steady. You gotta wait for daylight.

HOLLY: It's just an old watch battery, Miss Lena.

LENA: No it ain't. *She physically attacks Holly, slapping at her. Holly holds her off.* You don't want them to come do you? You're like everyone else. You're scared of them, ain't you? You don't want them talking to me.

HOLLY: You're crazy. You're just a crazy old woman. I was gonna help you, but you know what, I changed my mind. I'm going home. I thought I should be sorry for you with that old goat beating up on you, but now I don't care no more. You're crazy. You deserve what ever you get.

LENA: Bitch!

HOLLY: *(As she exits)* Lunatic.

Lena sits sobbing on the steps.

NANCE: Oh, come on, honey, it ain't so bad. We'll find it in the morning..

LENA: Why d'you bring her over here? Why d'you let her in my business?

NANCE: She wanted to help you. I mean, you gotta see how it looks to outsiders, Lena. That Joe Bob is a mean little bastard and you just let him beat up on you. I been watching it for years, the police come, they take him away, and the next day he's back again, and a couple a months later he does it all over again. I ain't never said much. I known you all these years and I kinda got used to it, but these young girls are different. They don't put up with no shit like that. Girls like Holly, they know their rights. They don't take nothing from no man.

LENA: I gotta stay. I told you.

NANCE: It's kinda hard to swallow.

LENA: *Putting her hand to her head.* I don't feel right without it.

NANCE: What do you mean?

LENA: When I'm wearing it, I get like a tingling - in my brain.

NANCE: All the time?

LENA: Yeah.

NANCE: It's been tingling in your brain since 1991?

LENA: I reckon.

NANCE: That's kinda a long time for a watch battery.

LENA: It ain't no watch battery. Look, I didn't tell you everything, not while that girl was listening, but there's something else.

NANCE: Oh yeah.

LENA: Yeah, I seen it on the television, one of them Specials they do, about UFO's and all, and they was talking to people, you know, people who'd seen aliens. Alien Abductions it was called. Did you see it?

NANCE: I don't think so. Bill used to watch them things, but since he's been gone, mostly I watch Reality Shows.

LENA: Well, there's these people talking about what they seen and what they felt, and when they was talking I realized they'd seen the same things I'd seen.

NANCE: But you didn't see nothing.

LENA: I didn't *remember* nothing, but that don't mean I didn't see nothing. When they was talking it all sorta flooded back into my mind. They showed drawings, you know, of the aliens, and it was like I recognized them, and some of them said the aliens done experiments on them, just like they done on me. And then I knew, I mean, I really knew, they was gonna come back one day, and they'd find me, and they'd take me away with them.

Pause ... The two women look up at the stars.

NANCE: *(Very seriously)* You really think so?

LENA: Oh yes.

NANCE: Would you go?

LENA: Yeah. Wouldn't think twice about it. Up there, flying up there among the stars. Think about it, Nance.

NANCE: I dunno. I mean, what if Bill came back and I weren't here?

LENA: You think I'm stupid staying with Joe Bob, well, it ain't no more stupid than you waiting for that Bill of yours. He ain't coming back. He's run out on you, Nance.

NANCE: He'll get tired of her one day.

LENA: Forget about Bill, he don't matter. Joe Bob don't matter. None of it matters when you got something else to think about. When they come for me I'm gonna go with them and I'm gonna be up there flying around among the stars, and I ain't never gonna think of Joe Bob ever again.

NANCE: You think they'd ever let you come back here, you know, when they was finished?

LENA: Don't want to come back.

NANCE: Never?

LENA: No. Ain't nothing to come back for. *She rises impatiently* I can't do this. I can't just sit here. I gotta do something. Suppose they come tonight. *She goes into the trailer.*

NANCE: Lena, what you doing in there, girl? You want me to come and help?

LENA: *Offstage* No, Nance , you helped me enough already.

NANCE: I'm sorry. Honest I am. Come on out here.

LENA: I'm doing something.

Nance moves downstage and looks up at the night sky. She shakes her   head, and then looks up again.

NANCE: No. No, it ain't nothing.

LENA: *Coming out of the trailer carrying a small and very dim flashlight* What you looking at? NANCE: I thought I saw a light up there.

LENA: Where?

NANCE: *(Pointing)* Up there?

LENA: It's them. It's them. I gotta find it. *She starts to search frantically through the bushes.*

NANCE: If I was with you, you reckon they'd take me?

LENA: *(Looking up at Nance)* You wanna go?

NANCE: I don't know.

LENA: I can't see nothing with this thing. *(banging on the flashlight)* Damn thing, ain't got no juice.

NANCE: Maybe it's just a plane.

LENA: And maybe it's not.

NANCE: *Coming over to help her* It coulda rolled under the trailer. Gimme that flashlight. Oh, this ain't no good. Ain't you got another one?

LENA: No, that's it.

NANCE: Can you still see the light?

LENA: *Looking up at the sky.* No. Oh yes, there. I seen it.

Now it's gone again. It keeps coming and going. You find anything?

NANCE: No.

Holly enters with a large, bright, flashlight.

HOLLY: Miss Lena.

LENA: Go away.

HOLLY: I come to help you.

LENA: You called me a lunatic.

NANCE: Hush up Lena. Here, gimme that flashlight.

Nance takes the light and continues to search in the bushes, Lena continues to look up at the sky.

HOLLY: What you looking at, Miss Lena?

LENA: We seen a light, up there.

HOLLY: I smelled something.

LENA: Oh yeah?

NANCE: That's McAllister's septic tank, I been smelling that all evening.

HOLLY: No, I smelled something else and it don't smell like no septic tank. What you reckon, Miss Lena?

LENA: Don't smell like no septic tank to me.

HOLLY: Yeah, but is it, you know, the same smell?

LENA: Maybe. *(sniffing)* Could be.

HOLLY: You reckon it could be angels?

NANCE: Or something else.

LENA: Keep looking, we ain't got long. Not if they be making a smell. *(turning to Holly)* So why did you come back? You beginning to believe me?

HOLLY: Yeah, well, no... I was just... well, I was thinking like...

LENA: Yeah.

HOLLY: I was thinking like my sister she believes in angels and there ain't no one thinks that's dumb.

NANCE: That's 'cause it ain't dumb.

HOLLY: And you, like, believe in aliens, so I guess that ain't dumb either. I mean, they're all hope, aren't they? All some kinda way to get out of here. Some sort of promise of better things.

NANCE: I found it.

LENA: Halleluia! Give it me.

She takes the device, puts it behind her ear and a look of peace settles over her face.

NANCE: You feeling anything?

LENA: Tingling.

NANCE: That all? They ain't talking to you?

LENA: Not yet.

NANCE: Maybe we missed 'em.

HOLLY: *(Firmly)* No, we ain't missed 'em.

NANCE: But...

HOLLY: We ain't missed 'em. Come on, Miss Lena, we'll sit out here and wait. There, you just sit down there and we'll wait together.

They all sit for a moment staring at the sky.

NANCE: We gotta look pretty stupid sitting out here sniffing McAllister's septic tank.

HOLLY: That ain't what we're doing. We're waiting for something.

NANCE: We're always waiting for something, ain't we?

HOLLY: Waiting and hoping.

Lena points to the night sky.
LENA: Look. A light.
They all look up hopefully.
NANCE: And there's another one.
HOLLY: Could be tonight.
LENA: Yeah, could be tonight.

CURTAIN

MARIO'S FINGERS
A One-Act Play
Finalist Pittsburgh New Works Festival
In a rundown bar an ambitious young woman rediscovers her true self
3m 1w

LOU:	The bartender (He's seen it all)
MARTIE:	A young man, untidy and cheerful
MARIO:	Tall, good looking but haunted
AMY:	A woman in her twenties. She looks conservative, but she isn't.
THE PLACE:	LOU'S PLACE, a rundown bar in a derelict steel town.
THE TIME:	Mid-winter, the present.

The setting is LOU'S PLACE, a rundown bar in a derelict steel town. At a minimum there should be a bar with bottles and glasses, several sets of tables and chairs and some sort of bar game, ideally a pool table, but a pin ball machine, or video game would suffice. There is an old payphone set off to one side.

At the opening, Lou is standing behind the bar, polishing glasses. He is grey haired and wears a bar apron. Two men are playing pin ball. One of them (Martie) is small, scruffy, long untidy hair, wearing a denim jacket and old jeans. The other, (Mario) is tall, and good looking. He wears a long, oversized overcoat, and a black satin baseball cap, worn backwards on his head. There are two glasses of beer balanced at the side of the pinball machine or game.

31

MARTIE: Did you see that? Did you? Did you? Am I great or what?

MARIO: Sure, sure, you're great. I owe you a beer.

MARTIE: Hey, Lou.

LOU: What?

MARTIE: Give us a couple more beers. On Mario.

LOU: I ain't no waiter. Come and get them yourself.

MARTIE: (*Crossing to the bar*) It ain't like you're too busy. It ain't like there's anyone here.

LOU: That still don't make me no waiter.

MARTIE: (*Crossing back to the pinball machine with a couple of cans of beer.*) Up yours, Lou.

LOU: Yours too.

MARIO: Leave it alone, Martie.

MARTIE: There ain't no call for him to talk to us like that.

MARIO: I said leave it alone. Don't go calling attention to yourself.

MARTIE: Sure, sure, whatever you say. Go on, it's your turn.

The two men return to their game and the focus turns to the bar door where a woman enters. She is late twenties, wearing a business suit, carrying a brief case. She looks around happily. She seems very much at home.

LOU: Amy.

AMY: Hi, Lou.

LOU: Long time no see.

AMY: I know.

MARTIE: Get on with it, man.

MARIO: Sorry.

MARTIE: You ain't concentrating.

AMY: Well, how do you like the new look?

32

LOU: It's different.

AMY: You don't like it.

LOU: I didn't say that.

AMY: You didn't have to.

LOU: It's okay. It's just that I ain't never seen you in a skirt, and your hair all done.

AMY: It's the new me.

LOU: There weren't nothing wrong with the old you.

AMY: Thrift shop clothes and army boots just don't make it in the real world, Lou.

LOU: I don't have nothing to do with the real world.

AMY: Yeah, well, we can't all be so lucky. I really came to use your phone, not to show you my new clothes.

LOU: Long way to come to make a phone call. I thought you'd have a smart phone or something in that briefcase.

AMY: I do, but you know Lou, there's no signal around here.

LOU: Yeah, that's what I heard. I like it that way.

AMY: So, I was in the neighborhood___.

LOU: Dressed like that? This ain't that kind of a neighborhood.

AMY: Don't give me a hard time, Lou. I have enough of that already.

LOU: Okay, if that's what you want me to believe, then I believe you. Make yourself at home, you always did.

AMY: Thanks.

She crosses to phone, hesitating as she passes Mario and Martie, still playing their game.

MARTIE: What do you call that man? That's shit.

MARIO: Hey, I'm doing my best. I've got problems you know.

MARTIE: Ain't we all?

33

LOU: You need change, Amy?

AMY: (*Dialling*) No thanks. I have it.

MARTIE: How could you miss that?

MARIO: I don't know. Unless I lost another one. (*Looking around on the floor}* Damn.

MARTIE : Some excuse, huh?

LOU: Hey, fellas. Keep the noise down. The lady's making a phone call.

Amy is looking at Mario with interest. He's on his hands and knees under the pin ball machine. She looks away to speak into the telephone.

AMY: Jay? It's me. Amy. Were you asleep?... Okay, okay, sorry I asked... I didn't mean anything. Honest, honey, I wasn't being smart. It's getting late, I just thought... Okay, okay. Could you look in my appointment book for me? It's in the bedroom. My phone? No it's dead..No, obviously if it was working I wouldn't have to ask you... Sorry. I don't mean to snap. Just look for it please. I need the address of my next appointment... Yes, of course I'm going... I know, I know. Yeah, I gotta keep pushing. Gotta keep focused. You don't have to tell me, Jay. I don't need you to tell me. I know what the bills are... Jay, Jay, shut up Jay!... I'm sorry, hon. I didn't mean to shout but I'm running out of change. Call me back, will you. Get the appointment book and call me back. I'm at Lou's... And why shouldn't I be?... Oh, don't be ridiculous. I haven't been here in years .... No I didn't. I just came in to use the phone... No I'm not. It was the nearest place, that's all... Call me back, Jay. Jay! Jay! Damn.

She hangs up the phone.

MARTIE: Pick it up, man, before I tread on it.

Mario picks up something from under the pin ball machine

34

and puts it in his pocket. They continue with their game.
Amy crosses back to the bar.

LOU: Everything all right?

AMY: Yeah, sure. I mean, nothing's perfect is it?

LOU: Ain't it?

AMY: Of course not. Look at this place, you wouldn't call this perfect, would you?

LOU: I do alright.

AMY: Not as well as you used to. You had a nice little business here once, didn't you - before they closed the Mill? That's what I heard.

LOU: I still got a business.

AMY: But not the same.

LOU: When did you get so interested in money?

AMY: When I found out how useful it is. You won't get any money here, Lou. All you do is collect drop outs and weirdoes.

LOU: I like weirdoes. I liked you when you was a weirdo, didn't I?

AMY: Yes, you did. And I'll always be grateful for that, but I really shouldn't be here now.

LOU: Now that you're respectable?

AMY: Married.

LOU: Married?

AMY: Yeah. Married.

LOU: No shit?

AMY: Two years. Jay.

LOU: The guy you brought here that one time. The prick in the suit?

AMY: Well you're right about the suit.

LOU: And the rest.

AMY: Not really. Not all the time. I'll take a Coke, please.

LOU: That all?

AMY: Yeah, I'm working.

LOU: You?

AMY: Yes, me. I gave up being a starving artist. It didn't pay the bills and Jay's ambitious. I mean, we're ambitious. We want things. Nice place to live, cars, that sort of thing.

LOU: That never used to worry you.

AMY: I was a kid, Lou. Anyway, I got a job with the IBA Business School.

LOU: What sort of a job?

AMY: Don't look at me like that. I can get a job, you know. I cleaned up pretty well.

LOU: Yeah, sure.

AMY: I'm an Admissions Representative. I go to homes of high school kids and talk to them about getting a career, going to School. It's a lot of evening work.

LOU: Tough sell?

AMY: I push hard. I mean, I figure I'm doing them a favor. They're kids. They don't know what to do with their lives. I'm helping them really. No good drifting, you know. I did enough of that myself.

Over at the pinball machine, Mario has pulled something out of his pocket and used it to stir Martie's beer. Martie yells in disgust.

MARTIE: Shit man, don't do that. That's disgusting. You wanna make me puke?

MARIO: It won't hurt you.

LOU: Keep it down, you two.

MARIO: I lost another one.

LOU: You sure it ain't catching?

MARTIE: I ain't caught it.

AMY: Who are they? They're new.

36

LOU: We got lots of new people, Amy. Those two are okay. Harmless really. The big one; he's in a bad way.

AMY: What do you mean?

LOU: Something weird. Real weird.

AMY: I'll keep out of his way.

LOU: That doesn't sound like you. You used to like weird things.

AMY: I used to shave my head, and make pictures out of dryer lint. Times change, Lou. I'll go and sit over by the phone. I'm waiting for Jay to call me back. I don't want to miss him. He gets impatient at times. Nothing bad, it's just that he wants me to do well. He wants me to make something of myself. He has to keep me on track. I don't seem to be able to do it by myself.

She crosses back to the phone. As she passes Mario their eyes meet briefly. She continues on her way, and sits down at a table near the telephone. She sets her Coke on the table.

MARTIE: Hey, come on. It's still your turn.

MARIO: I'm finished.

MARTIE: No you ain't.

Mario abandons the game and approaches Amy, with Martie close behind him.

MARTIE: Come on man. Don't start this shit.

MARIO: *(To Amy)* Hi.

AMY: Hi.

MARTIE: Yeah, Hi . *(Martie grabs something from Mario's hand and drops it into Amy's Coke.)* Here, lady, stir your drink.

Amy looks into her drink and leaps to her feet with a cry of disgust.

AMY: What the hell?

37

She knocks over the drink which spills onto the table. A finger falls out of the glass and lies on the table.
Oh my God. Lou! Oh my God.
MARIO: Pick it up, Martie.
MARTIE: *(Laughing)* Up yours, Mario. It won't hurt her.
AMY: It's a... Oh my God. It's a ...
MARTIE: Finger. It's a finger. Ain't you never been given the finger before?
MARIO: *(Bowing slightly)* Please, forgive my friend. He has no manners.
Mario attempts to pick up the finger but he cannot get hold of it. His right hand has only a thumb and a little finger. The actor should be able to create this illusion by keeping his fingers folded under and the sleeves of his coat should be overlong. Mario's crippled hand chases the finger around the table. He pauses, meets Amy's eyes.
AMY: I'm sorry.
MARIO: So am I.
Mario finally captures the finger and drops it into his pocket
MARTIE: Neat ain't it? It don't hurt a bit, and he don't bleed.
MARIO : We're bothering the lady. We should leave. *Instead of leaving he sits down at the table. He appears very confident.* Lou, bring the lady another Coke. She spilled hers.
AMY: No, no. I don't want any more.
MARIO: Please, sit.
AMY: No, really. I'd rather stand.
MARTIE: It ain't catching. I pick 'em up for him all the time. He don't always know when he's dropped one.

MARIO: (*Staring intently at Amy)* They grow back. Or at least, they used to.

AMY: That's nice.

MARIO: Sit down, please. You're looking very pale. I don't bite. *(He laughs)* I don't even pinch, not any more.

MARTIE: It's only fingers.

MARIO: (*Staring hypnotically at Amy)* Only fingers.

MARTIE: Not any other bits. Not any important bits.

MARIO: No important bits.

AMY: (Weakly) No, of course not.

She sits. Martie grabs Mario's left hand and holds it out under Amy's eyes. This hand should also appear deformed.

MARTIE: Look. He's growing new ones on this hand.

MARIO: No, I'm not. No good pretending. They've stopped growing.

MARTIE: Shit man, don't say that. Don't say nothing like that.

AMY: Have you -- er -- seen a doctor?

Martie drops into a chair on the other side of Amy and throws his hands into the air in disgust.

MARTIE: Doctors? Shitheads!

MARIO: I've seen doctors.

Lou crosses from the bar with a glass of Coke

LOU: They bothering you Amy? You want me to get rid of them?

AMY: It's okay, Lou. Really. You know me. I can look after myself.

LOU: I was only asking.

AMY: I'm okay. *She accepts the Coke* I'm waiting for my husband to call.

MARIO: There was no need for that.

AMY: I don't know what you mean.

MARIO: I wasn't going to hurt you. You didn't have to drag your husband into this.

AMY: I only said I was waiting for him to call. He's a busy man. I don't want to miss him. That's all.

LOU: Sure. (*Setting his hand on Martie's shoulder*) Don't do nothing else weird. Nothing else, you hear me? (*Lou returns to the bar*)

MARTIE: Hey, I ain't the weird one. I got all my body parts.

MARIO: So, you have a husband?

AMY: Yes, that's right.

MARIO *(Turning away)* I see.

AMY: But I didn't mean to offend you. I really am waiting for him to call.

MARIO: Of course you are.

AMY: This ... er ...condition of yours... I've never seen anything like it. Have you had it long?

MARIO: Long enough.

He looks at Amy's Coke. She pushes it towards him.

AMY: Go ahead, take it. I don't want it.

MARIO: No I don't suppose you do. You'll never look at a Coke the same way again, will you?

AMY: It wasn't your fault. Go ahead, take it.

MARIO: I can't.

AMY: Yes you can. Oh... I'm sorry. You can't, can you? Do you need a straw?

MARIO: Forget it. I don't want it.

AMY: How did it happen?

MARIO: I don't know. Perhaps it's a curse. I really don't know. It's something new. Unique. Maybe I'm just lucky, huh?

MARTIE: He didn't want to tell no one. Not at first.

40

MARIO: I thought it would go away, but it didn't.

MARTIE: So he starts looking for someplace to hide. I'm his cousin, three times removed or something, I dunno. Anyway he comes to me 'cause he don't wanna be seen no more. I tell him there ain't nobody he knows gonna see him on Mill Front Street. Ain't no one gonna go looking for Mario Amelio, Esquire, not here.

AMY: Esquire? You're a lawyer.

MARIO: Was.

MARTIE: Slick he was. Oh yeah. The brains of the family. There ain't no one done better than my cousin Mario.

MARIO: I don't want to be found.

AMY: But isn't there someone who could help you?

MARTIE: Hey lady, butt out. I'm helping him. I'm family, ain't I?

AMY: Professional help.

MARTIE: He didn't used to have nothing to do with me. Mr. Big Shot he was. We was nothing. We was the poor relations. It ain't the same now. He don't have no one else now.

MARIO: (*Looking down at his hands*) They're not growing back this time.

Amy makes a tentative gesture as if to touch his hands, and then withdraws

MARTIE: Give 'em time, Mario.

MARIO: I've given them time. What's next? Toes? Ears? (*He stands up*) The obvious?

AMY: Obvious?

MARTIE: (*Making an obscene gesture*) Yeah, lady. The obvious.

MARIO: I'm sorry. I know this isn't your problem. I saw you come in the door and even with the suit and the brief

41

case and everything, you looked so at home here, I
thought ... Oh, never mind what I thought. It doesn't
matter. As you so hastily told me, you're a married lady.
Come on, Martie, we're bothering people. I won't offer to
shake hands.

AMY: I'm sorry. It must be very difficult for you.

MARIO: It's not what I was expecting. I had it all once. I
lost it.

AMY: I've just found it. I don't want to lose it.

MARIO: Of course not.

AMY: I probably won't come here again. My husband
doesn't approve.

MARIO: I don't think he understands you.

AMY: That's a very old line.

MARIO: That doesn't stop it from being true.

AMY: Please, Mario, please understand. It's not personal.
It's nothing to do with your...

MARIO: Of course not.

MARTIE: Come on man, let's go if we're going.

MARIO: Yeah, sure.

*Exit Martie and Mario. Amy hesitates a moment and then
picks up the Coke. She takes a sip. She picks up the glass
and crosses to the bar.*

AMY: I'm ashamed of myself, Lou.

LOU: No need to be.

AMY: I wasn't very cool, was I?

LOU: It ain't easy.

AMY: When I first saw it, you know, the finger on the
table, I wanted to be cool. I wanted to pick it up and say
something easy, something polite.

LOU: Excuse me, sir, I think you dropped something.

AMY: Yeah, that's right.

LOU: I was the same, at first. All I could do was stare. I ain't bothered by it now, but I was then. I thought maybe I shouldn't let him in here, case it was catching, you know. But I let all kinds of weirdoes in here, it didn't seem right to keep him out.

AMY: You let me in didn't you? I was pretty weird.

LOU: You was just finding out who you were. Everyone's gotta do that.

AMY: I tried it all, didn't I?

LOU: Leather and chains.

AMY: Starving artist.

LOU: The macrobiotic shit.

AMY: Carbon neutral.

LOU: Marrying a prick.

AMY: Now wait a minute, that's not fair.

LOU: Career woman?

AMY: Stop it. Lou.

LOU: You wanted him, Amy.

AMY: No I didn't.

LOU: I could see it. There was sparks.

AMY: There's something wrong with him.

LOU: There's something wrong with all of us.

AMY: But not like that.

LOU: It ain't always that easy to see.

AMY: I don't have to listen to this.

LOU: No you don't. But in case you're interested... Over there, by the door. He dropped something.

AMY: Oh no, not another one. Poor man.

Amy crosses slowly to the door and stands looking at something on the floor.

I can't, Lou. I can't.

LOU: No one says you have to.

AMY: *(kneeling down)* It's one of the new ones. Oh, God, it's this little tiny finger. Like a baby's. *She touches it, tentatively.* It's so soft. So new.
The street door opens and Mario stands just inside, watching her. She doesn't see him. She closes her hand around the finger and gasps.
 AMY: Oh my God, it's holding on. It's holding me.
She looks up and sees Mario.
Let go of me, please. Please. I can't do this. I'm not strong enough.
The phone rings
LOU: Ain't that your call, Amy?
AMY: Let go of me, please. I have to answer the phone.
MARIO: I'm not holding you, Amy.
AMY: Yes you are.
She drops the finger suddenly, as though it has released her.
Oh.
MARIO: Go ahead and answer the phone. It's not your sympathy that I want.
Amy takes a couple of steps towards the ringing phone. Stops and turns.
AMY: He's going to be really mad if I don't answer right away.
She walks back, picks up the finger as though it were the most normal thing in the world, and hands it to Mario.
AMY: I think you dropped something, Sir.
Mario puts his arm around her shoulder and leads her to the door.
MARIO: Nothing important.
Exit Amy and Mario. The phone continues to ring. Lou crosses, picks up the receiver. He listens for a moment.

LOU: Amy? Amy who? Never heard of her. You got the wrong number, buddy.

CURTAIN

TWILIGHT
An Appalachian Ghost Story in One Act
First Place Winner Pittsburgh New Works Festival

Maggie Barnum falls off her bicycle into the arms of a man
who has been waiting fifty years for something to happen.

3M 1W

Cast

Peregrine Walton Daniels:	Aged 20 - Harvard graduate, and a member of Boston Society.
Maggie Barnum:	16 - a pretty, but educated girl from rural West Virginia
Jake Barnum:	Maggie's grandfather
Donnie McDillon:	Maggie's fiance.

ONE SET: A roadside in Appalachia.

TIME: The present

*The set represents a roadside in rural West Virginia. There is
a "Steep Hill" sign at the roadside with a couple of rocks,
large enough to sit on, a few straggly bushes. There is a bank
alongside the road and a ditch behind it. The bank should be
constructed in such a way that a person behind it is invisible
to the audience. It is towards sunset on a summer day. All is
silent except for the song of a lark off in the distance.*

*A man (PERRY) is standing in the road looking off into the
distance. He is a good looking young man dressed in 60s
clothing, but not hippie looking.*
The silence is broken by a piercing scream. A girl (MAGGIE)

46

on a bicycle hurtles across the stage, screaming. Perry jumps aside and she crashes into the bank and she and the bicycle disappear into the ditch. The scream is suddenly silenced. Perry stands as if uncertain what to do next.

MAGGIE: *(W. Virginia accent, from behind the ditch)* Shit. Goddamn. Damn, that hurts.
Perry stands still, not offering to help. Maggie emerges from the ditch. She's a pretty teenage girl in cut-off denim shorts and a tee shirt. She's brushing off dirt and twigs
MAGGIE: Well, thanks for your help.
Perry seems surprised, and looks around as though she might be talking to someone else.
MAGGIE: I said thanks for your help. Dammit, I near enough broke my neck down there.
PERRY: *(in an upper class Boston accent)* Are you talking to me?
MAGGIE: I sure am. There ain't no one else here for me to talk to.
PERRY: *(Looking around)* No, you're right, there isn't anyone else. You can see me, can you?
MAGGIE: Yeah, I can see you. I ain't blind.
PERRY: Are you alright?
MAGGIE: I think so. No thanks to you. What was you doing standing in the road?
PERRY: Did you see me?
MAGGIE: Of course I saw you. Leastways, I saw something, must have been you. Y'all are lucky I didn't run you down.
PERRY: Perhaps you should get your brakes fixed.
MAGGIE: I don't have no money for fixing brakes.
PERRY: No, I don't suppose you do.

47

MAGGIE: *(Rubbing her backside)* I reckon I've bruised my butt. *(Turning and showing Perry her backside)* Does it look bruised?

PERRY: *(Admiringly)* No, not at all. Really, it looks perfectly fine.

MAGGIE: Well it don't feel fine.

PERRY: *(Helping her down from the ditch)* Here, let me give you a hand.

MAGGIE: *(Checking herself out)* Man, I could have swore I'd be all banged up. Are you sure I ain't? What y'all staring at?

PERRY: I wasn't aware that I was staring.

MAGGIE: Well, you was. What's the matter? I'm hurt bad, ain't I? There's something awful you ain't telling me. Am I cut up bad? I'm scarred for life ain't I?

PERRY: *(Laughing)* No, no. I don't see any permanent damage. It's just that you've grown up a lot lately and you remind me of someone, that's all. Yes, you really do remind me of her.

MAGGIE: Well, you sure as hell don't remind me of no one. Except... no, not really. No, you don't remind me of no one. You're kinda cute though. How come you know so much about me? You ain't from around here. I ain't seen you before.

PERRY: But I've seen you, and your bicycle.

He looks into the ditch and then looks away hurriedly. He appears to be shocked.

MAGGIE: What's the matter?

PERRY: Oh, nothing. You certainly made a mess of that bicycle.

MAGGIE: *(Not looking into ditch.)* Oh hell. I'd sooner have broke my bones than broken that damned bike. He ain't never gonna forgive me for this. Not never.

48

PERRY: If you don't mind my asking, who is it that will never forgive you?

MAGGIE: My Grandpa. Shit. He's gonna beat me from here to next Sunday.

PERRY: Your Grandpa? You mean your grandfather?

MAGGIE: Yeah, my Grandpa. He's really gonna beat me.

PERRY: I don't think so.

MAGGIE: You don't know my Grandpa.

PERRY: No, you're right I don't. I must say that nothing appears to have changed around here. When all else fails, they beat up a woman.

MAGGIE: Spare the rod and spoil the child; ain't you never heard what the Bible says? It's his duty to beat me. I ain't got no Pa, not no more, so my Grandpa has to do it all. It's only right, it's his duty. *(Sighs)* He sure does like doing his duty. I gotta sit down, my legs feel weak. Oh shit, he's really gonna get me for this.

She sits carefully, remembering her bruises.

PERRY: I wish I could help you.

MAGGIE: You a mechanic? Can you fix it before he gets here?

PERRY: I'm good with my hands but.....

MAGGIE: But you ain't a miracle worker, I know. It'd take a miracle to fix that bike.

PERRY: *(Looking into the ditch again.)* It looks to me like it was pretty bad even before this last little accident.

MAGGIE: Yeah, well it's the only bike I got. It ain't had no proper brakes in months. This ain't the first time I've run off this hill. What about the beer?

PERRY: Beer! Do you have beer? I haven't tasted beer since...

MAGGIE: It ain't for you. It's for my Grandpa. There was a six pack in the basket. Are the bottles broken?

49

PERRY: (*Climbing down into the ditch*) Yes, I think you could say they're broken.

He climbs out with a broken beer bottle

MAGGIE: I always have to get him bottles, never cans. He won't have no cans even though they'd be much easier. Cans get shook up, but they don't bust. Now I gotta go home without his beer.

PERRY: You'll feel better in a minute. Sit quietly. Give yourself a chance. It's so nice to have someone to talk to. I've been waiting a long time for someone to talk to.

He sets the beer bottle down

MAGGIE: Y'all are staring at me again.

PERRY: I'm sorry, but you really remind me of someone.

MAGGIE: We all look alike round here. We're all related. This is Barnum Hollow and we're all Barnums.

PERRY: Yes, I know.

MAGGIE: Yup, Barnums, or McDillon's. Everybody's one or another.

PERRY: And which are you?

MAGGIE: I'm a Barnum. Maggie Barnum.

PERRY: Peregrine Walton-Daniels.

MAGGIE: Peregrine. What kind of a name's that?

PERRY: A terrible one. My friends call me Perry.

MAGGIE: You're not from around here?

PERRY: No, I'm from Boston. This is my first and last time in West Virginia. I didn't mean to stay. I was just passing through. I've finished up at Harvard and I wanted to see a bit of the country. I've been here a lot longer than I meant to be.

MAGGIE: I can't for the life of me imagine why. There ain't nothing here. Barnum ain't no more than a wide place in the road. It used to be something once, before the interstate passed us by, but now it ain't nothing. I'd leave in a minute, if I could.

PERRY: Would you really?

MAGGIE: No, not really. I'm all talk really. Shit, I wouldn't know where to go. I don't know nowhere but here.

PERRY: I don't know what they'd make of you in Boston.

MAGGIE: My Daddy left, years ago. He said he'd come back for me but he never did. I ain't never heard from him again. I guess he forgot all about me. Will you quit staring at me. Is there something wrong with my face?

PERRY: I'm sorry. I haven't seen anyone in a while, not to talk to.

MAGGIE: If anyone's doing any staring it should be me. I ain't never seen nothing like you before. Why you wearing them clothes?

PERRY: Don't you like them?

MAGGIE: They ain't exactly cool.

PERRY: On the contrary, they're very cool. They're summer weight.

MAGGIE: That ain't what I mean by cool.

PERRY: I'm sorry. I must seem very out of date.

MAGGIE: I dunno. Maybe you're the latest thing. We don't see much high fashion in Barnum Hollow but we got a satellite dish, so we get T.V.

PERRY: Satellite dish?

MAGGIE: Yeah, satellite dish. Don't look so surprised. We got a big one, HBO and everything. I've only seen clothes like yours in the movies. Yeah, I see movies. We ain't hicks, you know. We're civilized... What's the matter? You look like you don't know what in hell I'm talking about.

PERRY: What's a satellite dish?

MAGGIE: (*Standing up*) What's a satellite dish? What sort of dumb question is that? Don't go making fun of me, just 'cause I don't talk like them college girls. Just 'cause I ain't never been to Harvard.

PERRY: Oh, no, I wasn't doing that. I wouldn't dream of making fun of you. Don't you think you'd better sit down again?

MAGGIE: Yeah, I think I'd better. I don't feel too good.

PERRY: It's the shock.

MAGGIE: Shit, falling off that bike weren't no shock. I've done it before, believe me. Just so long as I ain't all scarred up. I'm getting married you see, and we're getting a photographer and everything. I been saving up. I want pictures I can show my grandkids. I'm gonna have a white wedding, and I don't wanna be all scraped up.

PERRY: You're not old enough to get married.

MAGGIE: I was sixteen last September. That's plenty old enough. Don't go giving me that look. I told you, it's a white wedding. I ain't knocked up or nothing.

PERRY: I never for one moment suggested that you were. You really are a very outspoken young woman.

MAGGIE: You was thinking it. I know what you was thinking. Well, let me tell you, I ain't let him near me. I've told him he ain't getting none till I got that ring. Why else would he marry me?

PERRY: I'm sure there are other reasons.

MAGGIE: I don't trust no other reasons.

PERRY: Why get married at all?

MAGGIE: I gotta get away from my Grandpa. I don't want another winter with Grandpa.

PERRY: It's all very sad.

MAGGIE: No it ain't. You sound like some old preacher. Shit,

I'll bet you ain't much older than I am, you just talk old. How old are you?

PERRY: Well that's not an easy question. I've tried to work it out watching the seasons come and go, but I may have lost a few years; there's been so many of them. As near as I can judge, I'm seventy.

MAGGIE: No you ain't. My grandpa's 70. You ain't no more than about 20. You think I just fell off the potato wagon?

PERRY: I've been here since 1968.

MAGGIE: No you ain't. What kind of a fool do you take me for? (*She tries to rise*) Oh, I feel real dizzy.

PERRY: Rest a while longer.

MAGGIE: Alright, I'll sit down for a minute, but don't y'all give me no more stuff about being 70 years old.

PERRY: You don't have to believe me if you don't want to. Just rest there for a minute. Tell me some more about this thing you were talking about. Satellite dishes was it?

MAGGIE: I ain't going along with this foolishness.

PERRY: Alright. Whatever you say. We have plenty of time.

MAGGIE: I don't got time to sit here with you. Donnie ain't gonna like it.

PERRY: Donnie?

MAGGIE: He's my fiancé. He don't like me talking to no strangers. And you being kinda cute and all, he wouldn't like that. He gets awful jealous.

PERRY: I don't think you have to worry about that.

MAGGIE: Donnie ain't real big, but he's tough, and he's mean. He'd mess you up pretty good.

PERRY: I don't think I'm in any danger from Donnie.

MAGGIE: I wouldn't want to see you get messed up.

PERRY: Wouldn't you?

MAGGIE: *(Flirting)* No. You got a nice face.

53

PERRY: You say what you think, don't you Maggie?

MAGGIE: I know what I like.

Voices offstage. They are the voices of Maggie's grandfather, Jake Barnum, and Donnie McDillon, Maggie's fiancé.

JAKE: *(Off-stage)* I don't know. Don't ask me. She's always late. She don't do nothing on time.

MAGGIE: That's them. That's Donnie and my Grandpa. We gotta get out of here. They ain't never gonna believe I only just met you. We've gotta get a story.

She ducks out of sight behind one of the stage props (not in the ditch)

DONNIE: *(Off-stage)* You ever take your belt to her?

PERRY: (*Looking offstage*) So that's Donnie. You can do better than that, Maggie.

MAGGIE: Come over here. Get out of their way.

JAKE: 'Course I do, but you can beat that one black and blue. It don't do no good.

PERRY: Who's that with him? It looks like... Maggie, is that your grandfather?

MAGGIE: It sure is. Get over here. He can be real mean.

PERRY: That's Jake Barnum.

MAGGIE: Perry, come on.

PERRY: Don't you worry about me, Maggie.

He sits down on the rock. Enter Jake and Donnie. Jake is a big, grey haired man in jeans and a dirty undershirt. Donnie is young, and scraggly with a bandana round his head. They are a very unattractive pair.

JAKE: Maggie. Maggie.

DONNIE: Hey! Yo! Maggie.

JAKE: She ain't here. Son of a bitch look at that.

He picks up the beer bottle which is next to Perry's foot. He apparently does not see Perry although Perry rises to his feet.

JAKE: That's my beer.

DONNIE: Hey, Maggie, where you at woman?

JAKE: Don't go hiding from me girl. You'll only make things worse for yourself.

Jake prepares to sit on the rock where Perry was sitting and for a moment they are face to face.

PERRY: Jake Barnum. Can you see me? Can you see me you bastard? Where's Laura? What have you done to her?

JAKE: I don't know why in hell you wanna marry that girl, Donnie. She ain't nothing but trouble.

He moves past Perry and sits down.

PERRY: Answer me, damn you. Where is she?

DONNIE: A man's gotta have a woman, don't he, and I'll get her straightened out. That's what God gave men belts for.

JAKE: Like I said, she don't respond to no belt.

PERRY: Try your belt on me, Jake. Go on try it. Why don't you take on someone your own size?

He begins to "box" but remains invisible to Jake.

DONNIE: My old man used to give the old woman a couple of good ones every Friday night, and he didn't never have no trouble from her. I ain't never tried it on Maggie, not yet. Didn't seem right, not before we was married.

PERRY: You and me, Jake, one on one. Come on.

JAKE: Her mom was soft with her. By the time I got her it was too late, she was spoiled. She ain't never listened to me.

PERRY: Come on. Fight like a man.

JAKE: She should have gone with her Pa. She still talks about him. Like he's gonna come back and get her.

PERRY: Come on dammit. Surely you can see me. Surely you can see something.

DONNIE: You think he might?

JAKE: No way. He ran off with some skirt from Wheeling. He ain't never coming back here.

PERRY: What did you do with my car? Did you keep it? Were you fool enough to keep it? Do you know what's in it, Jake Barnum?

DONNIE: So long as she don't take after him. I don't want no damaged goods.

JAKE: She ain't damaged. I keep my eye on her.

PERRY: I'll bet you do. You don't want it to happen again, do you?

Maggie has crept forward listening to the conversation, now she makes some small noise, disturbs a rock or twig; something slight.

DONNIE: Do you hear something?

JAKE: Like what?

PERRY: Like your past, breathing down your neck.

DONNIE: I dunno. I thought I heard something.

PERRY: What did you do to Laura? Why didn't she come?

JAKE: I don't hear nothing. (*Picks up the beer bottle*) I gotta teach her a lesson. She knows better than to drop my beer.

DONNIE: Maybe something's happened to her. Something bad.

JAKE: (*Rising*)There ain't nothing happened to her. She'll have some story or another. Always does. She's slippery Donnie. Slippery.

PERRY: Hey, come back. I'm not finished with you. Come back. Do you hear me? Come back.

DONNIE: (*Moving off stage*) Hey, Maggie, Maggie.

JAKE: Maggie, get your ass down here.

They exit.

56

PERRY: Damn. They couldn't see me. Maggie, Maggie, they're gone. You can come out.

MAGGIE: Go away.

PERRY: It's okay, Maggie, they're gone. My God, Jake Barnum, after all these years. Is he really your grandfather? That explains why you look like... Well, thank heaven you don't look like him.

MAGGIE: Go away.

PERRY: It's alright, really. They're gone.

He pulls her out into the open. She comes reluctantly, cowering away from him

MAGGIE: Don't touch me.

PERRY: Hey, it's alright. They're gone.

MAGGIE: (*Holding up her fingers to make a cross*) Get thee behind me Satan.

PERRY: Things haven't changed here, not in all these years. It's like time standing still... What's the matter, what are you doing?

MAGGIE: Casting out the devil.

PERRY: They're gone.

MAGGIE: Not them. You.

PERRY: I'm not the devil, Maggie. I'm Peregrine Walton-Daniels.

MAGGIE: You're a devil. I saw it. I saw with my own eyes. You made yourself invisible. You were right there with them and they couldn't see you. You made yourself invisible.

PERRY: (*Stepping towards her*) That doesn't make me a devil.

MAGGIE: Don't come no closer.

PERRY: I'm not going to hurt you,

MAGGIE: How did you do it? How did you make yourself invisible?

PERRY: I'm not really invisible, Maggie. I'm just, well, you could say that I'm just on another plane.

MAGGIE: You ain't on no plane. Go on, go away. Don't touch me.

She falls on her knees and begins to mumble the Lord's Prayer with her eyes tightly closed

PERRY: Maggie, please.

MAGGIE: Go away. You can't touch me while I'm praying.

PERRY: (*Sitting down*) Alright, I'll wait till you're finished. Take your time. We've got all the time in the world.

MAGGIE: (*Opening her eyes*) No we ain't. What do you mean?

PERRY: I think you're coming with me, Maggie.

MAGGIE: You gonna make me? You got demonic powers or something?

PERRY: Demonic powers? No, I don't think so. Although there's a lot of things I'm very unclear about. I do know that I'm a spirit.

MAGGIE: A spirit?

PERRY: Not a very happy one. You're the first person I've spoken to in 50 years

MAGGIE: What do you mean, spirit?

PERRY: A ghost.

MAGGIE: (*Poking him tentatively*) A ghost?

PERRY: Yes.

MAGGIE: (*Circling him with interest*) A ghost. I don't believe you.

PERRY: Then you tell me how I made myself invisible. You tell me why your grandfather, and that scrawny young man couldn't see me.

MAGGIE: Don't you go calling him scrawny. I know he ain't no prize but there ain't that many men around here.

PERRY: Don't change the subject. I was invisible, wasn't I?

MAGGIE: Well, yeah, you was. You sure was. (*She looks down the road in the direction that Jake and Donnie exited*) You was right in their faces and they didn't see you. A ghost, huh? An honest to God, ghost. How long you been here?

PERRY: Since 1968. What's that, about fifty, sixty years or so?

MAGGIE: And you've been right here, and no one ain't never seen you before?

PERRY: I've seen them. I've seen you on your bicycle, but no one's ever stopped before, not like you did.

MAGGIE: I sure did stop, didn't I?

PERRY: I guess I was in your way. I had just noticed for the first time how much you look like ...

MAGGIE: So you're a ghost. *She pokes him again.* You don't feel like no ghost.

PERRY: Perhaps you don't know what a ghost feels like.

MAGGIE: You sure are good looking, for a ghost. I mean you ain't got no bedsheet on, no blood dripping, no fangs, no nothing like that. You ain't bad looking at all.

PERRY: Well, you look pretty good too, Maggie. I like your clothes.

MAGGIE: These old things.

PERRY: Girls were a bit more... covered up in my day. Girls where I come from. I think there were other girls, especially California, but I wasn't allowed to see them.

MAGGIE: Why you here, Perry? Is it alright for me to call you, Perry? You don't have some special title, do you?

PERRY: No, no title. I like the way you say my name. It reminds me of... of someone.

MAGGIE: Why you still here, Perry? Shouldn't you have ...you know... moved on?

PERRY: I'm not ready to move on. I've been waiting for someone.

MAGGIE: Well, you ain't been waiting for me. I ain't coming with you. Forget that idea.

PERRY: No, you're not the one I'm waiting for. Huh, I've just realized. You're her granddaughter. If Jake Barnum's your grandfather, then you're her granddaughter. You look an awful lot like her.

MAGGIE: I've only got one grandma, and I don't look nothing like her. Granny Laura, why she's as wide as a barn, and she ain't got but a couple of teeth, and she's as crazy as a... Hey, don't look at me like that. What did I say? I didn't say nothing.

PERRY: Fifty years ago, Maggie, your Granny Laura was just as lovely as you are, and about the same age.

MAGGIE: My Granny. You're waiting for my granny?

PERRY: Yes, that's who I'm waiting for.

MAGGIE: That don't make no sense. She ain't even right in the head. I heard tell as how Grandpa Jake knocked her around something awful and...

PERRY: I knew I shouldn't have left her. I should have stayed with her. I should have faced him.

MAGGIE: Perry, what's the matter? Y ou've gone awful pale. You look awful. I mean, even for a dead guy you look awful.

PERRY: I'm sorry. It's not your fault, and you're not telling me anything that I didn't already suspect. If I could just go back and do it again...

MAGGIE: You and my Granny?

PERRY: The summer of 1966. I'd just graduated from Harvard and my mother wanted me to go to Medical School; she said I could beat the Viet Nam draft. So I only had a few weeks before I had to start.

60

MAGGIE: Viet Nam?

PERRY: I don't suppose you know much about it. I'm sure it's all over and forgotten years ago. But my mother was hysterical about my safety. You know how mothers are.

MAGGIE: I ain't seen my mother in...

PERRY: I decided to see America while I could. I had a new car, a Dodge Charger, bright yellow. It was a graduation gift. A real beauty. I had engine trouble on the way south from Wheeling, and I only just made it into Barnum Hollow. There was a service station at the crossroads. The only one for miles around.

MAGGIE: It's still there. That's where I live. With my Grandpa.

PERRY: Yes, I suppose you do. Is he still a lousy mechanic? I don't think he really knew what he was doing with my car. He told me I'd have to wait a week for a new part. Then he told me there was nowhere for me to stay. Then he said I could stay in his house, and charged me a small fortune for the privilege. I think he saw me coming.

MAGGIE: You stayed in my house, all those years ago?

PERRY: Yes, I did. I stayed in your house with your grandmother.

MAGGIE: Granny Laura?

PERRY: Yes,I stayed with Laura. I wasn't very happy about it. Barnum Hollow was a very dull place. There was nothing to do, not a thing, except watch the chickens scratching outside in the dust and talk to Laura.

MAGGIE: It ain't changed much, except there ain't no use talking Granny. She don't make much sense if you know what I... I'm sorry I don't mean to upset you. It's just that Granny Laura's been crazy as long as I can remember. She

61

don't do much but mumble, and she goes out to the chicken shed and sits in this old car and...

PERRY: What kind of car?

MAGGIE: Hell, I don't know. It's a big old yellow thing.

PERRY: Yellow.

MAGGIE: Yeah, with a real long hood, and lots of chrome.

PERRY: And leather seats?

MAGGIE: I reckon they must be. They ain't rotted or nothing.

PERRY: They're not ripped up?

MAGGIE: No, they're covered in chicken shit but...

PERRY: So he kept it. He kept it to remind her. He didn't dare drive it, but he kept it. Has anyone ever found...anything...in the car?

MAGGIE: Like what?

PERRY: Oh, nothing.

MAGGIE: Is it your car, Perry?

PERRY: Yeah, it's my Charger.

MAGGIE: It ain't much good now. I'm sorry.

PERRY: It's only a car.

MAGGIE: I expect it was real nice when it was new.

PERRY: Jake Barnum misjudged me, and he misjudged his wife. He went off and left us on our own. While he was waiting for the parts, he went off with his friends. He was gone a couple of days. Fishing he said.

MAGGIE: That's what they still say, but I don't never see no fish.

PERRY: Your grandmother was a lovely girl, Maggie, a bit like you, and just as outspoken. I was very uncomfortable with her at first. In Boston I'd pretty much kept to my own social class and your grandmother certainly wasn't the Boston social type. Oh no, she'd never have fitted in with my mother's friends. But after a while I didn't care. I knew we could find a place to be together. She didn't even need money to make her happy, just kindness. I don't think anyone had ever been kind to her before. I've been very ashamed of myself for a long time. She said he'd kill her if he ever found out, but I didn't believe her, and then, after a while, I didn't care. Neither of us cared, all we wanted was each other.

MAGGIE: That's real romantic, and real sad. You was like those people on the soap operas. You know star crossed lovers.

PERRY: We were stupid. We thought no one else was watching us, but I suppose they all were. All the Barnums and McDillons.

MAGGIE: Of course they was. There ain't nothing else to do.

PERRY: And I suppose someone told Jake when he came back. He didn't do anything, not right away. He acted like nothing was wrong. He kept me waiting another two days while he played around with my car. And at night I could hear him with Laura, It was just a little house and the walls were thin. I could hear everything he did to her. I wanted to kill him for what he was doing to her, but I waited. I waited for him to fix the car, and then I left.

MAGGIE: What do you mean you left? You mean you left her behind?

PERRY: No, but that's what I wanted him to think. I told her I'd come back for her. We had it all arranged. I took the car up over the hill here and walked back down. I waited for her here. Right here. Right where we are now. It was just getting dark, like it is now. I pictured her walking towards me through the twilight. I've been picturing her for fifty years. Coming out of the sunset, just like you did.

MAGGIE: She didn't come?

PERRY: No, she didn't, but Jake did.

MAGGIE: Shit.

PERRY: As you so delicately put it, shit. He's a big man, you know.

MAGGIE: Yeah, but you was, you know, fighting for the woman you love.

PERRY: That only works in fairy tales. It doesn't work against Jake Barnum's shotgun.

MAGGIE: He shot you?

PERRY: Yup. He shot me and he shoved me into that ditch. The same one that you... Maybe that's why...

Offstage conversation from Jake and Donnie

JAKE: So I says to the son of a bitch, that ain't no piston knock. Shit man, I know piston knock when I hear it.

MAGGIE: Grandpa.

JAKE: He says he ain't coming down a penny on the deal, so I says he can take his Chevy and shove it where the sun don't shine. *Enter Jake and Donnie. They completely ignore Perry and Maggie.*

MAGGIE: I'm sorry about the beer. I'll get you some more. See it was the brakes and....

DONNIE: She ain't here nowhere, Jake. I don't like it, her running off like this.

MAGGIE: Grandpa. Donnie. Hey, can't you see me?

JAKE: She's somewhere around. Maybe she's gone down to see to Laura. The old woman's been sick all summer and Maggie don't seem to like leaving her. Hope she ain't taken it into her fool head to give that old woman my beer.

MAGGIE: Perry, they can't see me.

64

PERRY: I know.

DONNIE: When she's my wife, she ain't gonna do no running around.

MAGGIE: Why can't they see me, Perry?

JAKE: She'll calm down, soon as you get her in the family way.

MAGGIE: Perry, why am I invisible?

DONNIE: You reckon?

JAKE: Sure. It worked with my old woman.

PERRY: (*Taking her arm*) It's alright, Maggie.

JAKE: She finished High School, you know. She's got papers.

MAGGIE: (*Breaking away and confronting Jake*) Papers! Papers! What am I, a pedigree cow?

DONNIE: Yeah. You know she's real smart, for a woman. She's got a real good head for figures. She's been saving her money and all.

JAKE: Well, don't go letting her into your wallet. Won't no good come of that.

PERRY: (*Taking her arm again*) Come on, Maggie.

MAGGIE: What wallet? He ain't got nothing in his wallet.

DONNIE: I wish I knew where she was. You don't reckon something's happened to her, do you?

PERRY: It's no good shouting, they can't hear you.

JAKE: We'll go ask the old woman.

DONNIE: You can't get no sense out of her. What's the matter with her anyway? It ain't, you know, what's the word? You know...

PERRY: It's not your concern any more. |

DONNIE: You know, when babies get born with the same thing their father's got. What's the word?

JAKE: I dunno.

MAGGIE: Hereditary, Donnie. That's the word you're looking for.|

DONNIE: *(puzzled)* Hereditary. Yeah, that's the word.

MAGGIE: Hey, he heard me. He heard what I said. Donnie, Donnie.

PERRY: Be careful, Maggie. Be very careful.

JAKE: No, it ain't hereditary.

PERRY: *(Confronting Jake)* Go on, Jake. Tell him what happened to her. Tell her what you did to my Laura.

JAKE: The old woman had an accident. Years ago, a little accident. She got hit by a Dodge Charger.

PERRY: The car. He used my car.

MAGGIE: Donnie, can you see me?

JAKE: What you staring at?

DONNIE: I dunno. I thought I saw something.

He reaches out towards Maggie, and she steps back

JAKE: There ain't nothing there.

DONNIE: No. I guess not.

MAGGIE: It's me, Donnie. Why can't he see me?

JAKE: We'd better keep moving. It'll be dark before long.

DONNIE: You don't reckon she's run off do you, like her old man?

JAKE: No. She's here somewhere. She's hiding. She knows I'll get my belt out.

Exit Donnie and Jake

66

MAGGIE: (*Calling after them*) Donnie, Grandpa. Perry, why couldn't they see me? Perry, Perry?

PERRY: *(Taking her hands)* It's alright. You'll be alright.

MAGGIE: No I won't. What's happened? (*She pulls her hands away and feels her face.)* I'm still here. I can feel myself.

PERRY: I can feel myself. That doesn't mean anything. You must be brave, Maggie.

He takes her hands again, leading her towards the ditch

MAGGIE: No, no. I don't want to look. Don't make me.

PERRY: It's alright. Really. She's very peaceful.

MAGGIE: She?

PERRY: Maggie.

Maggie looks down into the ditch. She is silent for a long moment

 MAGGIE: What's wrong with her?

PERRY: I don't know. It was a bad fall.

MAGGIE: *Tearful* That damned bike. It didn't have no brakes. I asked him to fix them. He was a mechanic, goddamit, you'd think he could fix the lousy brakes.

PERRY: It's over now, Maggie, and it's no great loss.

MAGGIE: It's my life.

PERRY: It wasn't much of a life, Maggie. All you were going to do was trade an old bully for a young one. You'd have been worn out before you were twenty five.   Come on. Come away.

MAGGIE: *Turning away* I hadn't even started. I wanted babies.

PERRY: It'll be alright.

MAGGIE: Will it? Will it really?

PERRY: Yes, it'll be alright. Don't cry.

MAGGIE: I ain't crying, not really. (*She sniffs*) What happens now?

PERRY: I'm not sure. I suppose we wait.

MAGGIE: What for?

PERRY: For Laura.

MAGGIE: Oh. (*Sitting down on the rock*) I suppose I should have known. I mean it looks different, don't it?

PERRY: You mean the sky?

MAGGIE: And the trees, and the grass. Everything. It's so bright. I ain't never seen the sky so blue. (*Sliding down so that she is leaning against the rock looking up at the sky.* It's real pretty.

PERRY: (*Sitting next to her*) Yeah.

SILENCE

MAGGIE: (*Sitting up again*) What's over there?

PERRY: I don't know.

MAGGIE: You mean you ain't never looked?

PERRY: No.

MAGGIE: Ain't you curious?

PERRY: No, not really.

MAGGIE: Oh.

Maggie picks up a stone and examines it. She is bored.

MAGGIE: So this is all we do?

PERRY: Huh?

MAGGIE: Now that we're ghosts, this is all we do? Just sit here?

PERRY: We're waiting.

MAGGIE: (*Standing up*) Maybe you're waiting, but I ain't. I'm going for a walk.

PERRY: I don't think you should. I'm not sure you'd be able to come back.

MAGGIE: I don't want to come back. Come on.

PERRY: I'm waiting.

MAGGIE: For crazy old Laura?

PERRY: Yes.

MAGGIE: (*Sits down again*) Laura ain't here, Perry, but I am. A bird in the hand's worth two in the bush, ain't it?

PERRY: I'm going to wait.

MAGGIE: (*Seductively*) But you said I look like her. Come on. Come with me.

PERRY: It wouldn't be right.

MAGGIE: Do you always do what's right?

PERRY: I try to.

MAGGIE: You're real uptight, you know that?

PERRY: I'm sorry.

MAGGIE: I bet you wasn't like this with your old Laura.

PERRY: (*Embarrassed*) I don't know what you mean.

MAGGIE: Yes you do. Shit, you're blushing. You got it on with old Laura, didn't you?

PERRY: That's none of your business.

MAGGIE: And you've been thinking about it for 50 years, haven't you?

PERRY: I've been doing no such thing. You are a very crude young woman.

69

MAGGIE: No, I ain't. I'm just normal. Go on, you can tell me. It was you and Laura, wasn't it, while the old man wasn't looking.

PERRY: *(Laughing)* Maggie, really!

MAGGIE: You did, didn't you?

PERRY: The nights were very hot, neither of us could sleep.

MAGGIE: No, I bet you couldn't.

PERRY: We were alone in the house. I couldn't help myself. One night I went into her room and...

MAGGIE: You ain't as green as you look, Perry.

PERRY: No, I guess I'm not.

MAGGIE: Come on.(*She tugs at his hands*) We'll go across that field there. It looks sort of bright over there don't it? Like something might be happening. Come on. Let's go and see.

PERRY: *(Rising to his feet)*I suppose it wouldn't hurt just to look.

MAGGIE: *(Taking his face between her hands)* You know what, you're cute. You're much better looking than Donnie.

PERRY: Maggie, you're just a child.

MAGGIE: No, I ain't.

Their lips almost meet and then Maggie pulls back, studying his face. Suddenly she removes her hands in a convulsive gesture.

No. No. You can't be. You can't be. Oh my God.

She releases Perry and runs over to the ditch, and disappears.

PERRY: What on earth's the matter?

MAGGIE: (*From the ditch*) Wait a minute. Wait there. I've got it here somewhere.

PERRY: Maggie, come out of there. Come on, we'll go for a walk.

MAGGIE: Wait a minute, goddammit. It's here somewhere. *She comes out of the ditch carrying a purse. She is rummaging through the contents.* You ain't never gonna believe this, Perry. Never in a million years. Oh where the hell is it? Here, here it is.

She produces a small photograph, dog eared and old.
Look at it. Look at it. Look at that face. I knew you reminded me of someone. I knew it. I knew it when I first saw you.

PERRY: (*Taking the photograph from her*) Who is this?

MAGGIE: That's my Pa.

PERRY: The one who ran away?

MAGGIE: Yeah, he went to Wheeling. He was always restless, always trying to get away, but he was my Grandma's favorite. You can see why, can't you?

PERRY: He has a nice face.

MAGGIE: A nice face. What the hell you talking about? A nice face! He's has your face.

PERRY: What?

MAGGIE: For a guy what's been to college, you're pretty dumb, you know that. That's your face.

PERRY: No, I don't think...

MAGGIE: Yes, it is. He's got your face. Shit, Perry, can't you see it? He's your son.

PERRY: No, I don't...

71

MAGGIE: You're my Grandpa.

PERRY: I can't be.

MAGGIE: Yes, you can. You and Granny Laura, and all those hot nights.

PERRY: She had a baby? My baby?

MAGGIE: Yeah, that's what it looks like. Not bad for a beginner, eh Perry?

PERRY: You think so? You think she had my baby? My baby. That's amazing. Oh, Maggie, that's the best news I've ever had. It's as though I'm not really dead. I have a son. I have a...a... a.... granddaughter.

MAGGIE: You old dog, you.

PERRY: Yeah, I guess I... Now wait a minute. Wait just a minute. (*He stands up very straight*) You watch your tongue young lady.

MAGGIE: I only meant...

PERRY: Let's have a little respect here. This is your grandfather you're talking to.

MAGGIE: Oh come on. You ain't serious.

PERRY: Of course I'm serious. I don't know quite what I'm going to do with you but...

MAGGIE: Lighten up, Perry.

PERRY: I don't think you should call me Perry.

MAGGIE: Well shit, I ain't gonna call you Grandpa.

PERRY: This will never do. We'll have to do something about the way you talk.

MAGGIE: The way I talk?

PERRY: The double negatives, the expletives, the frequent

scatological references.

MAGGIE: The what?

PERRY: The use of the word "shit" my dear, is not considered good form by members of Boston Society.

MAGGIE: But I ain't Boston...

PERRY: I am not... Don't say "ain't".

MAGGIE: I'll say whatever the hell I like. I ain't going to Boston. We're dead, Grandpa. Have you forgotten that?

PERRY: Shit!

MAGGIE: Ha! Feels good, don't it?

PERRY: (Rising and crossing to the ditch looking down) You know, Maggie, just for a moment there I thought I understood. I mean, I wasn't really dead, not if you were alive. But you're not alive, are you.

MAGGIE: No, I guess I ain't. I felt alive, until you told me I wasn't. You know, I think Donnie even saw me.

PERRY: He saw something.

MAGGIE: I know he heard me.

PERRY: (Climbing down into the ditch) Yeah, you're right. He heard you. Perhaps we're not too late. It can't end here, Maggie It can't be allowed to end.

MAGGIE: (Leaning over) What you doing to her?

PERRY: There's a pulse. It's not much, but there's something. Come down here, Maggie.

MAGGIE: No. I ain't going back.

PERRY: Maggie, you must.

MAGGIE: No, I ain't. I'm going over there, over where the sky's so bright. I wanna see what's over there.

PERRY: (Cl*imbing back out of the ditch*) Get back in there, Maggie.

MAGGIE: You can't make me.

PERRY: (*Grabbing her arm*) That's what you think. Go on, Maggie.

MAGGIE: Leave me alone. I'm not going back. I don't wanna go back. You were right, there weren't nothing to look forward to. I'll bet it hurts in there. I'll bet she's all beat up. I ain't going back.

PERRY: Maggie, dear girl, you're my heir, you're my stake in the future, you must go back.

MAGGIE: No, there ain't no future in it. I'm gonna stay here.

PERRY: You wouldn't have to stay in Barnum Hollow. You could leave. You could get an education. You could be anything you want to be. You've got good genes.

MAGGIE: Leave! How in the hell am I gonna do that? You ain't been listening, Grandpa. There ain't no way I can leave here.

PERRY: You could go to Boston.

MAGGIE: No, I couldn't. I couldn't never go to Boston

PERRY: Yes, you could and when you get there my family would take care of you.

MAGGIE: And how would I prove I'm your granddaughter?

PERRY: That would be difficult.

MAGGIE: Yeah.

SILENCE

MAGGIE:I feel real funny.

PERRY: I expect she's slipping away.

74

MAGGIE: Yeah, I expect so. I'm going for a walk.

She walks away towards the "light". When she is almost off stage Perry speaks again

PERRY: So you're going to let him win? .. Again?

MAGGIE: (*Turning back*) Who?

PERRY: Jake Barnum.

MAGGIE: Grandpa always wins.

PERRY: He's not your Grandpa. I am.

MAGGIE: Yeah, that's good ain't it? I'm glad to know that son of a bitch ain't really nothing to do with me. There ain't none of him in me.

PERRY: But if you don't go back, he's still won. He's wiped us out. Everything Laura did, carrying a child that wasn't his, keeping her secret, everything. It all comes down to you.

MAGGIE: I can't beat him, Perry, I've tried

PERRY: You could if I helped you.

MAGGIE: How you gonna help me? You can't even help yourself. Stuck in this old ditch for fifty years. There ain't nothing you can do for me.

PERRY: I can give you money.

MAGGIE: Ghost money? I wouldn't get far with that at the Greyhound Station.

PERRY: Real money. Money to buy you a ticket out of here.

MAGGIE: Enough to go to Wheeling and find my Pa?

PERRY: Enough to go to Paris and send Jake Barnum a postcard.

MAGGIE: Wouldn't that be something. Just to see his face. But you ain't got money. I mean if you took it out of your pocket and gave it to me now, I wouldn't have it, not when I got back.

PERRY: It's not in my pocket; it's in my car. Jake's been sitting on it all these years.

MAGGIE: You're kidding.

PERRY: No I'm not. That's why I asked you, about the car. If anybody had ever found anything.

MAGGIE: How much money?

PERRY: Quite a lot. Laura said I shouldn't keep it on me. She didn't trust the neighbors. So I hid it in the car.

MAGGIE: The yellow car?

PERRY: Stuffed inside the back seat. A diamond ring, diamond cuff links, my billfold.

MAGGIE: Diamonds!

PERRY: But I don't know if you'll remember. I don't know if you'll remember any of this. Will you remember me, Maggie?

MAGGIE: Diamonds! You mean we've been sitting on diamonds all these years, and old Jake don't know it.

PERRY: Maggie! Will you remember me?

MAGGIE: What?

PERRY: Will you remember me, Maggie?

MAGGIE: (*Maggie looks at his face for a long time*) I hope so, Perry. I want to. I want to remember that I'm yours, and not his.

PERRY: (*Returning to the ditch and looking down*) She looks like a strong girl. She's well built.

MAGGIE: I bet you say that to all the girls.

PERRY: Hey, I'm your grandfather.

Maggie climbs the edge of the bank

MAGGIE: I hope she's gonna be alright. Will you watch her...
Grandpa?

PERRY: I won't take my eyes off her.

MAGGIE: Thank you.

PERRY: (*Kisses her forehead*)All my hopes go with you, my
dear.

MAGGIE: I'll make you proud.

PERRY: I already am.

*Maggie climbs into the ditch and disappears from sight. The
light begins to fade and the bird song becomes louder. Perry
sits at the edge of the road, waiting.*

MAGGIE: (*Invisible*) Shit. God damn. Damn that hurts. Damn
bike.

*Maggie climbs slowly out of the ditch. She is scratched and
bruised and very weak. She cannot see Perry. She sits on the
rock, ignoring Perry.*

MAGGIE: Never again. He can get his own beer next time.

PERRY: Maggie, do you remember. Do you?

MAGGIE: I ain't never riding that bike again...

PERRY: Please, Maggie. Remember.

MAGGIE: (*Rising as if to walk away*) At least I ain't got broken
no bones. (*Pause ... puzzled.*) Don't have any broken bones.

PERRY: That's my girl.

Maggie looks around, as memory floods in on her.

MAGGIE: Perry, I wish I could see you.

Perry comes from behind her and put his hand on her

shoulder. She turns towards him.
I'm alright. I'm fine. (*She rubs her backside*) I've bruised my
butt... ass. Sorry, I don't know no polite word for it. (*She
looks around again*) Perry, I'll tell Laura you're waiting for
her. I'll tell her how pretty it was. I'll tell her it was real bright.
She walks away a few steps Goodbye, Grandpa.
She limps off stage as the sunset fades and the birdsong dies
PERRY: Thank you, Laura.
*Perry resumes his waiting position, but as the light comes
down, he looks off stage. His face brightens. He has seen
someone.*

CURTAIN

A CANDLE FOR ELVIS
ONE-ACT PLAY
Finalist Pittsburgh New Works Festival

Elvis Presley, or someone who looks a lot like him, returns from his exile on an alien planet to reclaim his throne.

CAST
3M 2W

MARY BIGELOW :   A woman celebrating her 70th birthday.

VIOLET SANSOM: Mary's married daughter, a dreamy, romantic, woman in her 30's

TED SANSOM :   Violet's husband, same age. Very businesslike, sucess oriented, uptight

ELVIS PRESLEY ?   Tall, grey haired, slightly verweight. Imagine what Elvis would look like if he were ALIVE today.

ELVIS IMPERSONATER: A young Elvis look-alike

ONE SET: THE LIVING/DINING ROOM OF MARY'S HOUSE.

TIME: THE PRESENT

The *living room of Mary Bigelow. Comfortably furnished with sofa, armchairs, and a dining table and chairs. Off to one side is an "Elvis Presley Shrine" with a velvet Elvis, statues, etc. and unlit candles. There is no one in the room someone is ringing the front door bell.*
VOICES OFF
VIOLET: Mom, Mom. Are you in there? Mom?

79

TED: Come on, Mary. Open the door.

VIOLET: Maybe she's gone out.

TED: Her car's in the garage.

Mary Bigelow enters from the bedroom with a suitcase. She's a woman of about 70, still attractive. She is laughing softly. She puts the suitcase on the sofa and then hears her visitors. She stands looking at the front door and listening to Ted and Violet outside. She stops laughing and looks faintly annoyed.

VIOLET: Perhaps someone gave her a ride.

TED: Who?

VIOLET: I don't know. One of the neighbors.

TED: Don't be stupid. She's in there. She's ignoring us.

Mary nods her head in agreement. She heads back towards the bedroom.

VIOLET: Ted, go and look in the kitchen window, please.

TED: You go and look.

VIOLET: But, honey, you're taller than I am. I can't see in.

TED: She's your mother.

VIOLET: Please.

TED: Okay, okay, don't nag me. Keep ringing the bell.

The doorbell rings again. Mary opens the bedroom door and speaks to someone inside.

MARY: Keep quiet. I'll see if I can get rid of them.

She closes the bedroom door and stands with her back to it protectively.

TED: There's no one in the kitchen. I don't have time to waste on this. Mary, Mary, are you in there?

The front door rattles.

VIOLET: Hey, it's open. She didn't even lock it.

MARY: Oh damn!

She opens the bedroom door again, and runs inside.

TED: Why couldn't you have thought of that before, instead of making us stand around out here?

The bedroom door opens again and Mary tiptoes out, heading towards the suitcase on the sofa.

VIOLET: I'm sorry. She doesn't usually leave the door open. It never occurred to me.

The front door opens and Mary scuttles into the bedroom leaving the suitcase on the sofa. Enter Violet and Ted. They are in their late thirties. Ted is well-dressed in business clothes and Violet bears a family resemblance to her mother, but has a rather dreamy, romantic, faded look.

VIOLET: Mom, Mom.

TED: The place looks different. She's done something.

VIOLET: She's always doing something, painting, wallpapering. She's constantly rearranging. I don't know where she gets her energy.

TED: I wish you had some of it. Anyway, she has nothing else to do.

VIOLET: She has her Elvis Club.

TED: Don't get me started on that. Why does my mother-in-law have to be President of the Global Elvis Remembrance Club? Can't she see how ridiculous that makes me look?

VIOLET: I've talked to her, dear, and she says that she doesn't care how it makes *you* look.

TED: Doesn't she care how it makes *you* look, she's your mother? Of course, you don't have an image to maintain, not the way I do.

VIOLET: I don't mind, and I don't suppose she'll stop now, not after all these years.

TED: She'll have to stop. If I get any higher in the company, she's going to be a real drawback. Do you think I want them to know who that I married into a family with an Elvis shrine in their living room? I'm not surprised you didn't ever bring me here before we were married. I suppose you didn't want me to think that insanity runs in the family. Hell, Violet, it's hard enough explaining you to people, without having to explain your Mom.

VIOLET: You don't have to explain me, Ted. There's nothing wrong with me.

TED: You could try to be a little more practical. You could try to hold down a job.

VIOLET: I do try. You know I don't want to be a burden to you.

TED: Well, try a little harder. She's not here, is she? Let's just put her birthday presents on the table and take off. You can call her later.

VIOLET: I guess you're right. At least we tried.

She places the presents on the dining table.

TED: (*Crossing to the Elvis shrine*) Wait a minute. Wait a minute. Look at that. I don't believe my own eyes. She's let the candles go out.

VIOLET: Oh dear, she never lets the candles go out. Do you think we should light them?

TED: Don't be ridiculous. Leave them alone. This might be it, you know. She might actually have started listening to me. Maybe she's getting better.

VIOLET: It's not a question of getting better, Ted. There's nothing intrinsically wrong with being an Elvis fan.

TED: He's dead, Violet. He's been dead for years.

VIOLET: So has Shakespeare, but you always say you're a Shakespeare buff.

TED: It's not quite the same thing, Vi. There are differences. For one thing, Shakespeare was a genius.

82

VIOLET: Mom thinks that Elvis was a genius.

TED: He was an ignorant, hillbilly joke, just like all those women in his fan club. Your mother's roots are showing, that's the problem.

VIOLET: Roots? I don't think so. I don't think she dyes her hair.

TED: Not hair roots, you nitwit. Family roots. You know, good ol' Southern roots.

VIOLET: Oh, yeah, I'm sure you're right. (*Crossing to the sofa and picking up the suitcase*) I wonder why she has this out. Do you think she's going away? Maybe that's why she put the candles out.

TED: If she's going to Graceland again, I'll shoot myself, or I'll have her locked up. How many times does she have to go there?

VIOLET: It's just something for her to do. She's lonely.

TED: If she'd just do it quietly it wouldn't be so bad. But all that weeping and wailing and seeing visions, it's embarrassing. If she gets her picture in the National Enquirer again, I know someone at the office will see it. I can just see them now, gathering round the water cooler. Hey, isn't that Ted Sansom's mother-in-law on the front page? See, the one with the sort of superimposed ghost of Elvis? Right next to Kim Kardashaian's alien space baby, and the 300 lb radioactive spider from Brazil?

VIOLET: Oh, Ted, relax. No one in your office would read the National Enquirer. I'm going to look in the bedroom.

She crosses to the bedroom door, opens it, looks inside and closes it again very quickly. She stands with her back to the door, just as Mary had done earlier.

VIOLET: (*Whispering*) Ted, Ted. She's in there.

TED: Good.

VIOLET: With a man.

TED: What?

VIOLET: A man. I couldn't see much of him, she was trying to hide him behind her, but I caught a glimpse of him. Sort of tall and grey haired.

TED: Does he have his pants on?

VIOLET: Ted!

TED: It's a reasonable question. Does he have his pants on?

VIOLET: I'm not sure. I didn't like to look.

TED: No, you wouldn't would you? Always the same, Vi. Still the same hang ups. There's nothing cute about a 35 year old shrinking Violet.

VIOLET: I'm not trying to be cute. I just don't like that sort of thing. Actually, I think he was putting them on. Oh, Ted, what shall we do?

TED: Nothing. If he's made her forget to light her candles to Elvis, I'm all in favor of him. I'm in favor of anything that will make her more normal.

VIOLET: Oh, I see. I suppose you're right. But what should we do?

TED: About what?

VIOLET: About her birthday presents.

TED: We should creep away, and leave her alone. It looks like she's already unwrapping her birthday present.

VIOLET: Ted, really, I can't think of Mom like that. And what about the suitcase?

TED: What about it?

VIOLET: Do you think she's going to ... elope?

TED: Elope? What are you talking about?

VIOLET: Oh, Ted, don't you see? I bet she wanted to surprise us. She's like that. She's going to run off and marry him.

TED: I don't know how you jump to such startling conclusions, Violet.

VIOLET: It's a talent of mine. I can read people's vibrations. I'm like that woman that we used to watch on Star Trek.

TED: I never watched Star Trek

VIOLET: Yes you did. You watched it with me all the time, even the reruns. So, you know who I'm talking about, the Counselor. The one with the black hair and the sexy costume.

TED: Star Trek's fiction ,Violet. You can't base your behavior on a character from Star Trek. Sometimes I think you're as nutty as your mother.

VIOLET: Ted, Ted, I feel it, I really do. I can feel the vibrations in the air. She's going to run off with him. Oh, it's so romantic. I wonder who he is.

TED: Run off? Like hell she is.

VIOLET: I know she is. The air is full of romance.

TED: I won't let her.

VIOLET: You can't stop her. She's perfectly free to do whatever she likes.

TED: She's not free to marry again, not while she has us ... you, to think about. We can't let her. We can't afford to let her.

VIOLET: I don't see why not.

TED: Because obviously he's after her money. It's quite a considerable sum, you know. Oh, I'll show him a thing or two. Mary, Mary. Mom!

VIOLET: Wait a minute. I thought you said it was a good thing.

TED: Yeah, well, I didn't think it through. I didn't think about our responsibility for your Dad's money. Mom. Mom. Come on out here. Mom.

85

VIOLET: Don't be angry with her, Ted, and don't call her Mom, she doesn't like it.

TED: Stubborn old woman. What does she know? I'm just standing up for our rights, your rights.

VIOLET: Oh, I don't care about the money.

TED: You will, when this gigolo has taken her for every penny she has, and you don't get your allowance any more. What if she loses the house and has to come and live with us, Elvis shrine and all? Do you want that thing in our house where everyone can see it?

VIOLET: It is kind of ugly, isn't it? Mom, Mom.

Mary opens the bedroom door and comes out, shutting the door firmly behind her.

MARY: Violet, Ted, how very nice to see you.

VIOLET: Hi, Mom, Happy Birthday.

MARY: What?

VIOLET: Happy birthday.

MARY: Oh yes, my birthday. Do you know, I'd quite forgotten.

TED: I'll bet you had. Who is he, Mary?

MARY: Who's who?

TED: The man in your bedroom.

MARY: Well, I don't know that it's ...

TED: He's after your money, Mary. Can't you see that?

MARY: No Ted, I can't see that, and I don't suppose you can either.

TED: You're planning to run off with him, aren't you?

MARY: Ted, dear, you mustn't jump to conclusions. That's not like you.

She crosses to the dining table and fingers the birthday presents.

Presents. How nice. Shall I open them now, or shall we have a cup of coffee first. Did you bring me a cake?

VIOLET: Well, no, I mean we meant to, and I did try to bake one, but it didn't come out right, and Ted said he'd order one but then ...

TED: I've been really busy at work, Mary, you're lucky I found time to be Here today.

MARY: I'm well aware of how lucky I am. I'll just go ahead and open the presents then, shall I?

TED: Mary, who is he?

MARY: None of your business, Ted.

TED: Yes, it is. If there's a man in your bedroom with his pants off, it's my business.

MARY: With his pants off! Who says he has his pants off?

TED: She did.

VIOLET: No, I didn't. I said that I couldn't tell.

MARY: Couldn't you, Violet? There must have been something missing in your education. Anyway, you're wrong. He has his pants on ... now.

TED: But he's had them off.

MARY: He had nothing at all on when he arrived. Is this present from you,

Violet? (Picking *up a gift*) It's very heavy. Let me guess. Something you made yourself?

VIOLET: Yes.

MARY: Then I don't suppose I'll ever guess what it is. Why don't you tell me.

VIOLET: It's this wonderful piece of wood that I found. It's not a log, it's more like a tree stump, and it had some really interesting fungus on it.

MARY: I see.

VIOLET: So I painted it, the fungus I mean, blue, to match

your kitchen. Your kitchen is still blue, isn't it? You haven't painted it again, have you?

MARY: No, it's blue.

VIOLET: Good. And then I took some dried grasses and spray painted them gold and ... and then I put some cup hooks on the side, so you could hang you know, things like ... things like...

MARY: (*Losing interest and putting down the present*) Like cups.

VIOLET: Yes.

MARY: Thank you dear, very thoughtful.

VIOLET: Aren't you going to open it?

MARY: Later dear. I think I'll have to work up to it. Your creations always take a little getting used to.

TED: Mom!

MARY: Don't call me Mom.

TED: Mary, what do you mean, he had nothing on when he arrived?

MARY: Nothing at all. Naked as a jay bird. It was quite a shock, I can tell you.

(She pauses, a look of great amusement crosses her face and she appears to make up her mind about something)
I recognized him immediately.

TED: Recognized him? How? What part of him did you recognize?

MARY: His face, Ted, his face. He hasn't changed a bit. All these years, but he still looks the same. Of course, I was already familiar with the computer aged pictures so the grey hair wasn't too much of a shock. I gave him some of Violet's father's old clothes. They're not what he's used to wearing. Her father never was particularly stylish.

VIOLET: So are you going to introduce us to him? Your new beau?

MARY: Oh, he's not my beau, dear. I would never be that fortunate. But he knows how loyal I've been and he appreciates loyalty. Of course, the candles were alight when he arrived, thank goodness. I don't know what would have happened if he'd come and found me not ready. It's a good thing that I've always been ready, isn't it?

Ted crosses to the Elvis shrine

TED: These candles? Are you talking about these candles?

MARY: Yes, of course I am. He blew them out himself. It was such a thrill, to see him do that and know that our long vigil is over.

TED: Mom ... Mary, what are you talking about?

MARY: Elvis, dear. He's come back. Elvis has returned to his people.

TED: Oh, shit.

VIOLET: Elvis? Oh, I don't think so, Mom. He's dead. He died in 1977. Remember, you went to Graceland to view the body? Remember? Why don't you open your present?

MARY: Well, it certainly looked like his body, but I know now that I was wrong. Elvis explained the whole thing.

TED: You're saying you have Elvis Presley in your bedroom.

MARY: I most certainly do. Would you like to meet him?

TED: Yeah, I sure would.

VIOLET: Oh, Ted, really, do you think we should?

TED: Don't be more of an idiot than you can help, Violet. Go ahead, Mary, wheel him in. I'd love to meet him.

MARY: I'll see if he'll come out. He's been away from people for a long time, he still a bit unsure of himself

Mary exits to the bedroom

VIOLET: Elvis Presley? Do you really think so, Ted?

TED: No, of course I don't think so. The man's been dead for years.

VIOLET: Mom never thought he was really dead. None of the fans thought he was really dead.

TED: Yeah, well, you know what I think of the fans.

VIOLET: I wonder where he's been.

TED: He hasn't been anywhere, he's not Elvis.

VIOLET: I know that. I meant that I wondered where he would say he's been. I'm not a complete idiot, Ted.

TED: You could have fooled me.

Enter Mary

MARY: He'll be right out. Dave's clothes aren't a very good fit, and he's very fussy about his appearance.

TED: So what's his story? Where's he been?

MARY: Story? Oh well, *(Looking very amused, as though she knows a secret joke)* I'll tell you what he told me. There he was, standing on my front door step, naked as the day he was born, and curling that top lip of his. There was no mistaking the way he curled that lip. Very polite, he was, called me Ma'am.

VIOLET: Did he?

MARY: Oh yes, he's real polite. He told me who he was, and of course, I didn't want to believe him, but he was very persuasive.

TED: And naked.

MARY: That too. Well, it seems that he was abducted by aliens.

TED: Aliens. Of course. Aliens. It's obvious.

MARY: They came to Graceland, and sucked him right up into their space craft, leaving behind only a hollow artificial shell, so no one would know what had happened. Then they took him to their planet.

VIOLET: What was it called?
Elvis enters from the bedroom
ELVIS: Well, Sugar, I never could pronounce it.

VIOLET: Is this him? Oh, Mom, he looks like him.
MARY: Mr. Presley, this is my daughter Violet.
ELVIS: Hi there, Violet. Did anyone ever tell you what pretty eyes you have?
VIOLET: No, I er...
TED: Vi, stop it.
MARY: And this is my son-in-law, Ted.
ELVIS: How do?
TED: I just want you to know that I don't believe a word of this nonsense. I don't believe in aliens, I don't believe in people being sucked up, sucked in maybe, but not sucked up, and I'm firmly convinced that Elvis Presley is dead and buried, which is a very good thing.
MARY: I didn't believe it at first, but the more you think about it, Ted, the more believable it becomes.
TED: To you maybe; not to me. Why would aliens want him?
MARY: For his brain. They wanted to study his brain. He was, after all, the most influential person on earth; far more influential than any of the world leaders.
TED: Mary...
VIOLET: There might be some truth in that, Ted. I'll bet you there wasn't a corner of the world anywhere, where they hadn't heard of Elvis Presley.
TED: They wouldn't take thirty years to study Elvis' brain, there wasn't that much of it left. You do know, don't you, that the man was completely blown away on drugs? A junkie.

ELVIS: Prescription drugs, son. Nothing illegal. Everything I took was prescribed by a doctor.

TED: You were a junkie. A dope head. A fat freak.

ELVIS: Son, it hurts me to hear you say that. You gotta remember , I have my black belt in karate.

TED: Look, you are not Elvis Presley, and don't sit there in my father in law's clothes, calling me "son".

ELVIS: Fashions sure have changed.

MARY: You'll be able to have your old clothes back, Elvis. They've all been preserved for you; and you look like you've lost a pound or two.

ELVIS: Sure have. I have to admit, I'd bulked up a bit there at the end, but I reckon I'm in pretty good shape now. I gotta get me some hair dye. This grey hair ain't gonna make it.

VIOLET: I don't know. I think it looks nice. Distinguished.

ELVIS: Thank you, honey.

VIOLET: It's my pleasure.

TED: Violet, shut up, you're making a fool of yourself. Now look here, you, whoever you are, why don't you just leave quietly, or would you like me to throw you out?

MARY: Ted Sansom, you have no right to throw anyone out of this house. This is my house, not yours. You sit right there, Mr. Presley, and take no notice of him. Would you like a cup of coffee?

ELVIS: Is there time?

TED: Before what?

ELVIS: Mary has to leave soon.

MARY: Do I?

ELVIS: Why you sure do. You promised.

MARY: Did I? Oh, that. I thought you were joking. You were joking weren't you?

ELVIS: No, I wasn't joking. I was serious. I need your help, Mary.

MARY: *(Whispering to Elvis)* This is great. Okay, okay, I'll go along with it. *(Aloud)* I'll make some instant coffee, it won't take a minute, and then I'd better finish packing my stuff if they're coming to get me.

TED: Who's coming to get you?

MARY: *(Heading for the kitchen)* The aliens. They have to have someone to replace Elvis, surely you understand that. They're not going to let him come back unless they have someone to take his place. Elvis thought of me because he knew I was the president of his fan club. He knew I'd understand that he had to come back. He knew that I'd understand that the new generation has to have the chance to see him in person. Recordings just aren't good enough, Ted. Surely you realize that now that you've met him in person.

She exits to the kitchen

TED: Mary, come back here. Don't be so ridiculous. Mary. *He follows her into the kitchen, slamming the door behinhim. There is a long silence during which Violet stares at Elvis, nervously.*

ELVIS: *(Singing under his breath)* You ain't nothing but a hound dog, crying all the time.

VIOLET: Stop it, stop it. Don't do that, there's no need.

ELVIS: I gotta see if I still got a voice. They wouldn't let me sing, up there.

VIOLET: Up there on the planet with no name?

ELVIS: It had a name. I just can't pronounce it.

VIOLET: You don't have to pretend with me. I know Ted treats me like an idiot, but I'm not that stupid. I get vibrations, but that doesn't make me stupid. I know you're not really, Elvis... are you?

ELVIS: Ain't I?

VIOLET: No. This is some game that you and Mom have cooked up, isn't it, to put us off the scent? But you can't put me off that easily. I know what my vibrations are telling me. You're eloping, aren't you?

ELVIS: No, I don't think so, but your ma 'll be leaving in a few minutes. I hope she don't change her mind. I got a lot of catching up to do.

VIOLET: You can trust me, you know. I'm not like Ted. I don't mind what Mom does so long as it makes her happy. All Ted worries about is money. What's going to happen to Dad's money? Will there be any left for him? He's always been like that.

ELVIS: Your ma's a nice lady. I feel kinda bad about her, but I don't know what else to do. I gotta get back to Graceland and take care of my affairs. I don't even know whose spending my money.

VIOLET: It's alright, really it is. I've been wishing and wishing that Mom would meet someone. Her life is so dull, with nothing but her Elvis Club and her card parties. Actually, if you don't mind me saying so, I think she's done pretty well for herself. I mean, you're really quite a good looking man... for your age, and you do have this sort of magnetism about you, that I can't quite explain. My mom said that's what the real Elvis had. She saw him, you know, a couple of dozen times.

ELVIS: She wrote me my first ever fan letter. 1954

VIOLET: You?

ELVIS: Elvis, she wrote to Elvis. It was real cute, real sweet. She heard me on the radio.

94

VIOLET: She told me she wrote to you, but I didn't know that was your first ever letter... I mean Elvis's first ever letter. Mom was just a teenager, and she said she heard this fabulous song on the radio, and she just had to write. She said she couldn't explain what happened, but she just knew she had to write to you ... to Elvis. She was only a kid.

ELVIS: It was a big event for me getting that there fan letter, my first one. It was always kind of special. I kept it. I wish I didn't have to do this to her.

VIOLET: How did you know really know about the letter? Did Mom tell you? That's it, isn't it? Mom told you.

ELVIS: She didn't have to.

VIOLET: You are not Elvis Presley.

ELVIS: (*Looking across the table at her, their eyes locked*) Ain't I?

Long pause

VIOLET: If you're Elvis, then who's buried at Graceland?

ELVIS: It's a shell, honey. These people got technology you and me can't even begin to figure.

VIOLET: What people? Little green people?

ELVIS: No. They're big, and kinda blue.

VIOLET: What do you really want?

ELVIS: I wanna go home, darlin'. I wanna go back to Graceland. It's what I want and it's what your ma wants. She wants the King to come back to his people.

VIOLET: All right, you don't have to trust me if you don't want to, but you're not fooling me. And I know you didn't have any pants on. I looked.

ELVIS: Oh?

VIOLET: I really looked.

95

ELVIS: Good for you, darlin'

The kitchen door opens and Mary enters, followed closely by Ted

MARY: I don't want to hear any more about it. I'm going and that's final. Violet dear, what do you think I should take? You're so much better at packing than I am. I mean, I don't know what the weather will be like.

ELVIS: It's real warm. I wasn't never cold.

MARY: So I won't need my winter coat?

VIOLET: Come on Mom, the game's up. I've been talking to this man, whoever he is and ...

MARY: He's Elvis Presley, dear.

VIOLET: Mom, there's no need to do this. If you want get married again, just go ahead and get married, you don't have to go through all this.

TED: Mom, about the bank account...

MARY: You'll be all right, Violet, honey. You're a grown woman now, even if you don't act like one. Mr. Presley says they'll leave behind an artificial body, just like they did for him. That way you can say that I died. I've left everything to you in my will. To you, Violet, not to Ted. Oh, Elvis, I really should warn you about Priscilla.

ELVIS: What about Priscilla?

MARY: Well, you've been gone a long time, and she's had a whole life, you know. Been in films, and all sorts of things. Been married a couple of times. So when you see her again, she might not be quite as you remembered her.

VIOLET: But she still looks good. She's a blonde now. I guess it hides the grey hair.

ELVIS: A blonde? I can't see her as no blonde. Her and me we both used the same hair dye you know.

MARY: What I'm saying is that the world's changed a lot

since you've been gone, and you won't be able to pick up where you left off.

ELVIS: No problem. Me and Priscilla, we were through.

MARY: And, of course, your daughter's been married over and over again. I don't know who she's married to now, but I do know she even married Michael Jackson, which we, in the club, thought was very strange. I don't know why she did that, and they didn't stay married for more than about five minutes.

ELVIS: Michael Jackson?

MARY: He's was a singer. Big star. They called him the King of Pop.

ELVIS: No. I'm the King.

VIOLET: He's gone now. Or, I suppose he is, unless he was up there with you.

ELVIS: Wasn't no one up there with me. The King don't share.

MARY: About Lisa.

ELVIS: I heard you, she married this King of Pop?

MARY: But he died. She's been married a couple of times. She has children.

ELVIS: My little Lisa with children. Imagine that. Wait a minute, wait a minute, that makes me a ... that makes me a granddaddy.

MARY: Well, yes it does.

ELVIS: I can't be no Granddaddy.

MARY: It's all right, it's all right. Your fans won't mind. We're all used to the idea now.

ELVIS: Oh, I don't know.

MARY: They still love you, Elvis. They even put your face on a United States Postage Stamp.

ELVIS: Is that right?

MARY: Sure is.

Violet has been looking in Mary's suitcase and now she pulls out an old flannel nightgown

VIOLET: Mom, is this what you're taking?

MARY: It's comfortable.

VIOLET: But Mom ... not for this.

MARY: Not for what?

VIOLET: Mom, come on. I know you all think I'm pretty naive, but I do know a few things. *(She lowers her voice)* Don't you have anything a bit more ... sexy?

MARY: Sexy? Why would I want anything sexy? But you may be right, Mr. Presley did say it was real warm up there.

VIOLET: Alright, Mom, you can play it that way if you want to, but you're not fooling me. You're eloping, aren't you?

MARY: No, I am not.

VIOLET: It's okay. I approve. In fact I think he's rather attractive. He's has a sort of magnetism.

MARY: Of course he does.

VIOLET: In fact I would say that you've done pretty well for yourself, and he does look a bit like Elvis Presley.

MARY: He is Elvis Presley. You know, you're right. I don't want to take this old thing with me. I have that new one Aunt Alice gave me when I was going to have my gall bladder operation. I never wore it in the hospital ... too flashy for a hospital. Maybe I'll take that.

VIOLET: *(Continuing to look through the suitcase)* You need help, Mom. You've packed all the wrong things.

MARY: I was very rushed, and I had my mind on other things.

VIOLET: I know. I saw.

MARY: I guess I was excited. It was all so unexpected. And I don't really know what the place will be like. I haven't been able to think straight since he arrived; and he couldn't help me much because he didn't have any clothes at all.

VIOLET: Do you want me to come and help you?

MARY: Oh, Violet, would you?

VIOLET: Sure, Mom.

Violet and Mary exit to the bedroom

TED: So, how much do you want?

ELVIS: For what?

TED: For clearing out and leaving my mother in law alone.

ELVIS: Hey, man, I don't want nothing. I'm outta here anyway. You think I wanna be around when they come back?

TED: When who comes back?

ELVIS: Them folks that snatched me and looked at my brain. I don't wanna see their ugly blue faces ever again. No, no, I'm gonna put a few miles between me and them. Your ma-in-law said she'd let me have a few bucks, to see me on my way. Few bucks so I could fly me to Graceland.

TED: Ah, now we're getting down to it. A few bucks? How many?

ELVIS: I don't know. What's air fare these days? I hear inflation's been something pretty bad. I guess a plane ride's real expensive. Couple of thousand?

TED: I don't carry that kind of money.

ELVIS: That's cool, man, you don't have to give it to me if you don't want to. I ain't forcing you. I'll wait for Mary to come back in and see what she thinks.

TED: Ah, I see. Now we're speaking a language we both understand, aren't we?

ELVIS: Are we?

TED: I think so. A thousand?

ELVIS: You reckon that's enough?

TED: Fifteen hundred, and you never come back.

ELVIS: I don't usually mess with small bills.

TED: Okay, okay, two thousand.

ELVIS: Better write it for cash. I don't got no identification or nothing.

TED: I bet you don't.

He pulls a check book out of his pocket and starts to write

Who thought up the Elvis Presley thing, you or Mary? It was so stupid I almost believed it; and I think you really had Violet suckered in there for a minute or two. Of course, Vi, isn't too big in the brains department.

He looks Elvis in the face and hands him the check

You do look a little like him. The eyes, the mouth, something, I can't quite put my finger on. I guess that's what Mary saw in you.

ELVIS: Thanks, son, this is mighty generous of you.

TED: Don't call me son.

ELVIS: About these clothes of your daddy's.....

TED: Keep them.

ELVIS: But they're your.....

TED: I said keep them. I don't want them, not after you've had your hands on them. Just get out. Go on, you got what you came for. Go.

ELVIS: I should say goodbye to Mary. Tell her what to expect when they come. They don't really mean to hurt but ...

TED: Drop it. There's no one coming.

ELVIS: There sure is.

TED: If anyone comes, I'll be waiting, and I won't be pleased to see them.

ELVIS: You'll be waiting?

TED: Yeah, me.

ELVIS: You? Yeah, you. Ha, I never thought of that. You.

100

Yeah, I wouldn't feel bad about that. I was beginning to feel bad about Mary, she's a nice lady.

TED: Why don't you just get the hell out of here; you've got what you came for.

ELVIS: (*Waving the check*) More than I came for. Ciao, son.

TED: Don't call me son.

ELVIS: See you later, alligator.

TED: Get out of here.

ELVIS: (*Crossing to the front door and singing "Blue Suede Shoes"*)

Well, it's one for the money, two for the show, three to get ready and go man go, etc.......

TED: Get out. *He slams the door behind Elvis.* He even sounds like him. Mary, hey Mary, Violet. Come on out here.

MARY: (*From inside the bedroom*) In a minute.

TED: (*Crossing to the bedroom and opening the door*) Now, Mary. You can leave the packing. You won't be going anywhere.

MARY: (*Coming from the bedroom followed by Violet*) What are you talking about, Ted? I'm going to this planet, whatever it's called.

TED: I got rid of him, Mary.

MARY: You what?

TED: I got rid of him. He was after your money, Mary. I don't know what sort of a line he gave you, but believe me I know his type, they home in on pathetic widows like you and ...

MARY: Pathetic widows? Is that how you think of me, a pathetic widow?

TED: A pathetic, rich widow, Mary, an easy target for someone like him. You have to be more careful, or that money will slip right through your fingers. Perhaps you should give me a power of attorney.

MARY: What did you say to him?

TED: Not much. We understood each other perfectly. It was a man thing.

MARY: Oh, of course.

TED: I named a price and he took it.

MARY: You did what?

She sounds very amused. Ready to laugh

TED: I named a price. Two thousand bucks, Mary. That's you're going price.

VIOLET: Ted, how could you? Oh poor Mom. They were going to elope.

MARY: (*Laughing*) Oh, I don't think so.

VIOLET: Mom, you don't have to be brave, not for me. I understand.

MARY: You're a good girl, Violet. Your heart's in the right place, but you don't understand, dear. You don't understand at all. So, Ted, he got two thousand dollars out of you. That was clever. I could never have done it.

TED: I don't see what's so funny.

MARY: No, I don't suppose you do. Humor never was your strong point.

TED: Mom, he wasn't Elvis Presley.

MARY: Of course he wasn't. I may be a pathetic widow, but I'm not a complete moron. He was a male strip-o-gram.

VIOLET: A what?

MARY: For my birthday. I'm betting the girls in the card club sent him over. It's my big one, seventy. They knew I needed cheering up, so they found a retired Elvis impersonator. Well, he's certainly cheered me up. Watching him get two thousand dollars out of Ted Tightwad is the best birthday present I could ever have had.

VIOLET: Mom, a male stripper. How gross.

MARY: Oh, grow up, Violet. Actually, you couldn't really call him a stripper. He didn't have to strip, he was stark naked when he arrived.

TED: I don't believe this.

MARY: I hustled him inside pretty quick, I didn't want the neighbors to start talking. And the girls had given him this story to tell, about how he was Elvis Presley and he'd been abducted by aliens. I don't know the last time I had such a good laugh. But he was a nice man. Really, a nice man. I have to call the girls and thank them. He really gave them their money's worth. I loved the way he stuck to his story after you both turned up. That was way beyond the call of duty.

VIOLET: But Mom, he was in your bedroom.

MARY: He didn't have any clothes with him. I don't know where he left them. I mean, a joke's a joke, but enough is enough. I couldn't let him come out naked, not after you arrived.

TED: But the suitcase.

MARY: It was old clothes for the Salvation Army. You're right, Violet, if I was slipping away for a dirty weekend, I'd take something a little different.

VIOLET: Oh, Mom. I'm disappointed.

MARY: Disappointed. Why's that?

VIOLET: I thought... I hoped ... you were eloping. He was so nice, and, well, sort of ... sexy.

MARY: He was, wasn't he? Reminded me of the real Elvis.

VIOLET: (*Starting to laugh*) And you gave him two thousand dollars to go away?

TED: Shut up, Violet. It's not funny.

VIOLET: But it is. You fell for it. You of all people.

TED: I never thought he was Elvis.

103

VIOLET: But you thought that Mom had believed him. You thought it was a big trick to get Mom's money. That's because you can't think of anything else. Money, money, money.

TED: Shut up, Violet.

MARY: Oh, cheer up, Ted. It's not the end of the world. At least I won't have to be taken away by aliens.

VIOLET: I didn't know you had two thousand dollars, Ted. Where did you get two thousand dollars?

MARY: Leave Ted alone, dear. He's had a hard day. I tell you what we'll do. We'll all go out and have a drink to celebrate my big birthday. I've been dreading it you know. No one likes to think they're growing old, but thanks to Mr. X this has been the best day I've had in years. Come on, Ted. It's on me.

TED: I don't want a drink. You and Violet go.

MARY: Oh, come on, Ted. Don't take it so hard. So you made a fool of yourself, it happens to everyone.

TED: Not to me.

MARY: All right, we'll go without you if that's how you feel.

VIOLET: Do you think we should?

MARY: Yes, Violet, I think we should. I think you and I should go somewhere quiet, and talk about this money that your father left me. I think we should talk about who it belongs to, and who's going to spend it. Come along, dear.

TED: Mary, now wait just a minute.

MARY: Too late, Ted. Oh, I have to do one more thing. I have to light the candles. *She crosses to the shrine and lights the candles.* It gave me quite a turn to see him blowing out those candles. They haven't been out since the day the King died. I don't think he should have done that. (*Laughs)* But it was worth it. Goodnight, Elvis.

She picks up her purse and Mary and Violet cross to the front door

MARY: Goodnight, Ted.

VIOLET: Goodnight, Ted.

Exit Violet and Mary.

Ted glares angrily after them and then goes across to the shrine and blows out the candles.

TED: Goodnight, Elvis.

The front door rattles. Ted looks round guiltily.

Okay, Mary. Okay, I'll light them again.

He lights a match

About that bank account, Mary, I was thinking that if you put it in my name.....

The front door opens and an Elvis impersonator comes in carrying a CD player. He switches it on, and Hound Dog begins to play.

IMPERSONATOR: Hi, Happy Birthday. Are you Mary?

TED: No, I'm not Mary. Do I look like a Mary?

IMPERSONATOR: Well go get Mary, son. I'm ready to rock and roll.

The Impersonator is by now beginning to strip to the music

TED: Hey, stop that. What are you doing?

IMPERSONATOR: I'm just doing my job, son, just doing my job.

TED: Wait a minute. Wait a minute, if you're the impersonator, then who......

The final scene depends on the production budget, ideally a large blue humanoid should enter the room, but a satisfactory effect could be created with a blue light

TED: Hey, hey, what are you doing? Get away from me. No, no, I don't want to come with you. I'm a married man. I have responsibilities. Mary, Violet, Elvis, someone. Help.

105

Ted is dragged protesting from the room as the impersonator continues to strip and the music swells to a crescendo

CURTAIN

WAR BRIDES
First place winner Pittsburgh New Works Festival

A WW2 soldier lives on the dreams of what might have been, and a war bride only wants to forget

3W/3M

CAST

VERA	An Englishwoman in her sixties
JACK	An American man in his sixties
YOUNG VERA	An English girl in her late teens
YOUNG JACK	A young American Soldier
SYLVIA	An English girl in her late teens
NICK	A young American Soldier
VERA'S MOTHER	A formidable, elderly

Englishwoman.

Time is 1980 and 1944
The place is New York City and also Dover, England.

At the opening, the stage is set with a card table covered by a white cloth, a British flag is pinned to the cloth as a skirt. Several plates of cakes and cookies on the table. Two folding chairs.
Vera, a well-kept woman in her sixties is standing behind the table. She wears a sensible but not unflattering tweed suit.
Enter Jack. He is also in his sixties. He is dressed in expensive looking casual clothes appropriate for the 1980's.

Vera speaks with a British accent.
VERA: Would you like to buy some cakes or cookies, sir?
JACK: No thanks, I don't think......
VERA: It's for a good cause.

JACK: I'm not really much of a cake eater and ....

VERA: We are the British Women's Club of New York City, sir. We support many local charities. Would you like some chocolate chip cookies?

JACK: British Women's Club. Really? *He moves closer to the table.* I was there in the war.

VERA: *(Wearily)* Were you really?

JACK: Oh yes. I know about English girls. *He winks and nods suggestively*

VERA: They all say that. How about some home-made bread?

JACK: Sausage rolls. Do you have any sausage rolls?

VERA: No. I'm sorry sir. The health department won't let us serve meat.

JACK: No sausage rolls. I used to like them. Of course with all the rationing and everything, I don't know what kind of meat they were using. Still, they tasted okay. What do you English say "A bit of alright?"

VERA: Yes, that's what we say. But you see, there's a chance of food poisoning when you try to keep them warm and the Health Department...

JACK: Yes, yes, of course. I see what you mean. I was over there, you know, in 44. Stationed in Dover. Sometimes it seems like yesterday.

VERA: Not to me.

JACK: Were you a war bride? No, you're too young.

VERA: Thank you, but yes, I was a war bride.

JACK: Those were the days weren't they?

VERA: Yes, I suppose you could say those were the days. If you will excuse me.....

JACK: Dover. I remember Dover.

He sits. Vera looks around for another customer. Seeing no one, she sits, resigned to having to listen to him.

CROSSFADE

*Two pools of light, opposite sides of stage. Jack stands in
one, Vera stand in the other. They remain in the pool of
light during this scene and subsequent scenes employing
this lighting. They take no action, but are obviously
spectators.*

*Young Jack enters in uniform alongside old Jack. Young
Vera enters alongside old Vera. Young Vera wears a tight
fitting 40's style dress. SOUND Glenn Miller playing
"Moonlight Serenade".*

*Young Jack whistles, young Vera responds to the whistle but
not to him. They do not see or communicate. Nick enters
alongside Young Vera. Nick is also a young soldier in
uniform. Sylvia enters alongside Young Jack. She is young
and very pretty in a romantic fashion and dressed in 40s
style evening gown.*

*Young Jack and Nick are American GI's. Nick speaks with a
New York accent. Sylvia appears to be very upper class
British.*

YOUNG JACK)
NICK   )   Well, hi there.

YOUNG VERA:)
SYLVIA   )   Hello.

YOUNG JACK)
NICK   )   Have we met somewhere before?

YOUNG VERA:)
SYLVIA   )   I don't think so.

NICK: I just thought I'd ask

YOUNG VERA: Don't you know a more original opening line?

YOUNG JACK Are enjoying the dance?

SYLVIA: Yes, it's very nice.

NICK: Do you wanna dance?

YOUNG VERA: Don't mind if I do.

Young Vera and Nick dance, embracing tightly.

YOUNG JACK: Would you like to dance?

SYLVIA: I don't really know you.

NICK: You gotta name?

YOUNG VERA: Yes, soldier boy. I've got a name. First you tell me yours.

YOUNG JACK: If I were to introduce myself, would you dance with me?

SYLVIA: I'll think about it

NICK: I'm Nick

YOUNG VERA: I'm Vera

YOUNG JACK: I'm Jack

SYLVIA: I'm Sylvia

Young Jack and Sylvia dance very formally. Young Vera and Nick continue to dance very close together.

CROSSFADE

Lights up on Jack and Vera sitting at the card table.

JACK: I was eighteen years old, green as grass, never been out of Toledo. It was all so new, so exciting

Jack is not listening to Vera, he is lost in his memories, but Vera is listening to him.

VERA: Not for me

JACK: I remember how it felt just to walk down the street. Everything so different, like nothing I'd ever seen. The children used to come running up and asking "got any gum chum?", thinking I was special, a cowboy or something. And the girls, always smiling. With all the

110

troubles they had, they still smiled at us. I guess we were a novelty.

VERA: And a necessity.

JACK: All the guys said English girls were easy. They thought it was their patriotic duty to comfort the troops.

VERA: If there was anything in it for us.

JACK: It wasn't as easy as they said.

VERA: *(Stands)* You must excuse me. I really must try to sell some of these baked goods. We have to raise funds, you know, for charity.

JACK: No. Please don't get up. I'm enjoying talking to you. It's bringing it all back.

VERA: Maybe you want to bring it all back. I don't.

JACK: Did I tell you her name was Sylvia? She was the classiest lady I'd ever met.

VERA: Well, you hadn't met many had you?

JACK: I knew she was special the minute I set eyes on her. She had this air about her. I can't explain it. She seemed so, I don't know, aristocratic.

VERA: Nick had an air about him. Oh what a way he had with girls.

CROSSFADE

Lights up in left pool. Young Jack and Sylvia are dancing. Glenn Miller is playing. With each appearance Sylvia's dress becomes more romantic, as Jack paints her in his memory.

YOUNG JACK: Do you come here often? I'm sorry, that's real corny. I'm not very good at small talk.

SYLVIA: No, I don't.

YOUNG JACK: Don't what?

SYLVIA: Come here often... Mummy and Daddy don't like me to come. Of course, I know the war has really broken down a lot of social barriers which is actually a very good thing, but Mummy and Daddy still don't like me to mix with the villagers.

YOUNG JACK: What are you, a lady of the manor or something?

SYLVIA: No, not exactly, or at least, we don't call it a manor anymore. Mummy and Daddy went away for the weekend, so I just sneaked down to see how the other half lives. They'd be just livid if they knew I was dancing with a Yank. hope no one tells them.

YOUNG JACK: Are you sort of aristocracy? Like royal blood or something?

SYLVIA: Very diluted royal blood.

YOUNG JACK: Imagine that, Jack Voegel dancing with an aristocrat

Left lights down, right lights up. Nick and V era are still dancing..

NICK: So you're Vera. My buddy Chuck said he met you here and you were really something.

YOUNG VERA: Really, he said that?

NICK: Sure, he said you were real friendly.

YOUNG VERA*: (stepping back)* Watch it. I don't like what you're saying.

NICK: I didn't mean no offence. We like friendly girls. We get lonely over here, not knowing no one. We like girls who are real friendly.

YOUNG VERA: I remember Chuck. He gave me stockings. Two pairs. Silk ones.

NICK: Plenty more where those came from.

YOUNG VERA: And chocolate, and a pound of tea. I took it home for my mum. She doesn't get much and she misses her tea.

NICK: Of course she does. Wanna take a walk outside. Look at the moonlight?

YOUNG VERA: I dunno. Maybe. Where are you from Nick?

NICK: Me? Oh New......California.

YOUNG VERA: New California. I've never heard of it.

NICK: Oh sure. That's the part of California that's right alongside the ocean. It was the last part of California to be settled so that's why they call it New California.

YOUNG VERA: Oh. I don't know much about America; only what I've seen at the pictures. Is it really like that? You know, swimming pools, and orange groves, and servants?

NICK: Sure babe, just like that.

YOUNG VERA: Is everybody really rich?

NICK: Sure, everybody's really rich. Just like in the movies. You wanna go for a walk now?

YOUNG VERA: Maybe. Are you rich Nick? Chuck said that he had a ranch and horses and everything.

NICK: Well, I don't have a ranch, but I've got a house in California with a swimming pool and orange trees growing by the pool. You can reach right out of the water and pick a fresh orange right off the tree.

YOUNG VERA: Really? It sounds wonderful. I'd love to see it.

NICK: Just stick with me honey.

YOUNG VERA: Really! You'd really show it to me!

NICK: As soon as we've settled this business with Hitler. You wanna go look at the moon?

YOUNG VERA: Sure, Nick. Your own swimming pool. Really?

CROSSFADE TO LIGHTS UP ON JACK AND VERA AT THE TABLE.

VERA: I don't Want to talk about this anymore. These are painful memories.

JACK: Oh, no, don't say that. I've kept Sylvia alive in my mind for 40 years. Those were wonderful days.

VERA: Wonderful. I lost my father, my brother and two boyfriends. It's alright for you to talk about the good old days, you weren't hungry and scared. You didn't have to sleep in a bomb shelter every night. I lost six years of my youth in that war, and I'll never get them back.

JACK: I'm sorry. I didn't mean to upset you. I appreciate how hard it was for you. I know that Sylvia wasn't eating properly. She was so thin and pale, almost like something out of a dream.

VERA: That's what she was, something out of a dream.

JACK: No, no. She was real. I danced with her that night. I held her in my arms and she was real. She wouldn't let me take her home. She said the servants might see me, but we arranged to meet again.

VERA: Servants! She was bloody well making it up. She was just like anyone else. She was playing a little game with a Yank who was too wet behind the ears to realize what she was doing. If she Didn't want you to take her home, it was because she lived in an ordinary house. Just like the rest of us.

JACK: Boy, are you bitter. What do you have to be so bitter about?

VERA: Bitter. I'm not bitter. We all had our bit of fun with the Yanks, but we weren't all as lucky as your Sylvia. Some of us had to pay for our good times.

CROSSFADE TO RIGHT LIGHT UP

Young Vera stands alone in the light. She is wearing a coat and a headscarf. In the background someone whistles "Lili

114

Marlene" Enter Nick

NICK: What are you doing here?

YOUNG VERA: You got my message then?

NICK: Yeah, I got your message but you don't know what I had to do to get out here. We're all confined to barracks you know.

YOUNG VERA: Yes, I know. It's all the talk down in the village. This is it, isn't it? The big one? You're going over.

NICK: I can't tell you that, not that I even know for sure. But it looks like it, Babe. It looks like action at last.

YOUNG VERA: I had to see you.

NICK: To say goodbye? Hey, don't worry, I'll be back. They'll have trouble catching old Nick Rossi. Don't you worry about me, I'll be okay.

YOUNG VERA: But I had to see you.

NICK: You just can't get enough of it can you? Come on over here.

YOUNG VERA: That's not what I came for.

NICK: Come off it. You love it, you know you do. You can't get enough of me, admit it.

YOUNG VERA: It looks like I've already had too much of you.

NICK: What's that supposed to mean?

YOUNG VERA: I think I'm in trouble Nick. You know, pregnant.

NICK: No, no, you can't be. I was careful.

YOUNG VERA: Not careful enough. I'll have to tell my mother, and she'll have to tell you commander and...

NICK: Now hold on a minute. Take it easy, honey. When I get back, we'll sort it out. Yeah, that's what we'll do. When I get back. Sure, sure. I'll even marry you, you know, do the right thing. You can trust me, babe. Don't say nothing now, just wait till I get back. I'll make everything right.

115

YOUNG VERA: How do I know you'll come back?

NICK: I said I'd make it right, didn't I? So stop worrying, okay? Just think about those orange groves, and those California swimming pools. We'll get married and we'll have our own house, Spanish ranch style, and we'll get a Nanny for the baby and you'll live in luxury. It'll be like your wildest dreams come true. Look, I've gotta get inside now.

YOUNG VERA: Do you love me, Nick?

NICK: Sure, I do. Of course I do and when I get back, I'll take care of everything. I have to go now.

YOUNG VERA: Don't you want to kiss me?

NICK: Oh, yeah, sure. *Kisses her briefly.* I'll see you when we get back. Don't worry about a thing.

YOUNG VERA: And we'll really go to California?

NICK: Sure we will. Sure we will. You, me, and the baby. Don't worry about a thing.

CROSSFADE TO LEFT LIGHT UP.

Sylvia is standing alone wearing a shawl and flowers in her hair. Young Jack enters.

YOUNG JACK: Oh, you waited, I wasn't sure you would.

SYLVIA: I felt I should give you a few minutes more. I know you have important duties.

YOUNG JACK: Well, not so very important. I'm only a corporal, you know.

SYLVIA: I know. If you were an officer, I might be able to talk Mummy and Daddy into meeting you, but a corporal ... They just wouldn't hear of it, I know.

YOUNG JACK: Don't you ever think of defying them?

SYLVIA: Oh no. I couldn't do that. They've been through so much. Shall we sit here on the beach? I like to listen to the waves breaking on the pebbles.

Young Jack spreads his jacket and they sit together on it, staring out to sea.

SYLVIA: Tell me about America.

YOUNG JACK: What's to tell? To be honest, I haven't seen much of it.

SYLVIA: I understand it's very large.

YOUNG JACK: Compared to Britain, yes it's enormous.

SYLVIA: One of my uncles went to America, I believe. Uncle Nigel. He was a sort of black sheep. I understand my grandfather wanted him to go to the colonies, but Uncle Nigel insisted on going to America. New York, I think, or maybe somewhere in California. I'm not really sure. We don't talk about Uncle Nigel. Perhaps he'll make his fortune and come back to rescue the family from ruin.

YOUNG JACK: Is your family ruined?

SYLVIA: Oh yes, I think so. They're all dead you see. Cut off in the flower of their youth.

YOUNG JACK: Your whole family?

SYLVIA: All the young men. We lost a whole generation in the First World War and now we're losing another generation. There's no one left, just old men and girls.

YOUNG JACK: You've lost everyone?

SYLVIA: Everyone who counts. There's no one suitable left for me to marry. If I were just an ordinary girl I could marry an American, but I'm not ordinary. Some girls are so desperate, that they'll marry anyone, just anyone.

YOUNG JACK: And you're not desperate?

SYLVIA: (*Rising suddenly*) No, of course not, and anyway I could never make an unsuitable marriage. Daddy and Mummy would be devastated, just devastated. I have my duty to consider.

CROSSFADE TO LIGHTS UP ON TABLE

Jack and Vera seated at the table.

VERA: Somehow this lady love of yours doesn't ring true. Are you sure you're remembering it properly?

JACK: Of course I am.

VERA: Perhaps over the years you've sort of .... well ... embroidered it a bit. She sounds like someone out of a novel.

JACK: Don't judge everyone by your standards.

VERA: What are you implying?

JACK: Perhaps you're trying to excuse your behavior by saying that everyone behaved the way you did.

VERA: What would you know? So you met some stupid girl who gave herself airs and graces and had a Mummy and Daddy at home to make sure she didn't come to any harm. It wasn't like that for me. I had to make my own way. I did what I had to and I'm not ashamed of anything.

JACK: I wasn't trying to offend you ... I just don't want you to spoil my memories.

VERA: Yes, well, you live with your memories and I'll try to live without mine.

CROSSFADE TO LIGHTS UP ON RIGHT POOL

Vera is with her mother. Vera is wearing a maternity smock. Vera's mother is a formidable elderly lady in a sensible dress and a ridiculous hat. She appears grim and determined. Church organ music playing in the background.

YOUNG VERA: I'll be okay Mum. There's no need to upsets yourself.

MOTHER: I'm not upsetting myself. I'm just determined that this young man should do the right thing by you. Where is he, that's what I'd like to know?

YOUNG VERA: He'll be here.

MOTHER: I hope so. It's not decent you walking around

118

like that without a wedding ring . What were you thinking of Vera?

YOUNG VERA: I was just trying to find some happiness.

MOTHER: Stuff and nonsense. If we all went around trying to find happiness, a fine state the world would be in. Seeing as how he got you in the family way,you'd think he'd be a bit more eager to marry you.

YOUNG VERA: He'll be here.

MOTHER: If I hadn't gone up to the barracks myself and seen his commanding officer myself, he probably wouldn't ever have come back. It was just a stroke of luck that he got himself wounded and had to come back here. Now he can marry you before the baby's born. We've never had any bastards in our family, and we're not going to have any now, not if I have my way.

Enter Nick in uniform, arm in sling, bandage around head.

MOTHER: So, there you are, and about time too.

NICK: Afternoon Ma'am. Hello Vera.

YOUNG VERA: Hello, Nick.

MOTHER: Well, let's get on with it then, the Vicar's waiting. You don't seem to be very eager about this young man.

NICK: Oh yeah, I'm eager, of course I am. It's just that I'm not feeling well. My wounds ...

MOTHER: Never mind your wounds. All you have to do is stand up in front of the Vicar and make an honest woman of my daughter. Then you can go back to hospital for all I care.

YOUNG VERA: I was hoping we'd have a bit of a honeymoon.

MOTHER: You've had your honeymoon by the look of things. You got the cart before the horse and now you're paying for it. I hope you're happy over there in America.

119

NICK: She can't come to America right away, you know. I don't know how long it will take before she can come. It might be years. That's what I hear. It might be years before any war brides can be sent

MOTHER: If it takes years, then it takes years. I don't care, just so long as you send her money.

YOUNG VERA: I'm looking forward to it. It'll be a whole new life. Not like living in this crummy place. We'll live in California and have our own house and a swimming pool and ...

MOTHER: I'll believe it when I see it. First you get in there and get married. Well then, boy, take her arm. No need to look like you're frightened to touch her, not after what you've done to her already.

YOUNG VERA: Tell me you love me, Nick.

NICK: Sure, sure, I love you.

MOTHER: Good, now let's get you married.

CROSS FADE TO YOUNG JACK.
Jack is consulting his watch. Enter Sylvia in old work clothes.

YOUNG JACK: I thought you'd never get here.

SYLVIA: I had to slip away when no one was looking.

YOUNG JACK: (*kisses Sylvia's hand*) But these clothes, and your hands... they're ... dirty.

SYLVIA: (*snatching hand away*) I'm sorry, I didn't want you to see me like this. It's my war work. All the men have gone to war and I'm helping on the farm. I take care of the sheep. I had to bring them with me. The whole flock is just down the road. I can't leave them alone long or some hungry family will turn them into lamb chops.

YOUNG JACK: You poor darling. Life is so hard for you.

SYLVIA: No, no, it's nothing compared to the sacrifices others are making. My cousin, Rowena, she has to take

120

care of the pigs. Can you imagine that? At least I was spared that job and the sheep are really rather lovable in their own wooly way. But it is very hard on the hands.

YOUNG JACK: *(kisses her hand again)* After the war is over, perhaps I could ...

SYLVIA: No, no. Don't even speak of it. I know what you're going to say and I couldn't, I simply couldn't. It's my duty to stay here and help rebuild my shattered country.

YOUNG JACK: It's people like you who make me understand why I'm over here fighting this war.

SYLVIA: And we do appreciate it, Jack, we really do. I know that some of the ... other girls ... express their appreciation rather more ... physically ... but you understand I wasn't brought up that way.

YOUNG JACK: Oh, I would never ask you to ... I mean, I know that you have standards and I have mine ... I wouldn't suggest that we ... oh no. You're perfectly safe with me.

SYLVIA: I know I am. I only wish Daddy thought the same way. He says that Americans are only after one thing.

YOUNG JACK: If only I could meet your father, I could explain. Perhaps I could just drop by accidentally. I could pretend I was out for a walk and I'd lost my way. If he met me he'd know I wasn't a sex fiend.

SYLVIA: Really, what a thing to say.

JACK: I'm sorry. Do you realize that I don't even know where you live. I don't even know your last name.

SYLVIA: Some things are better if they remain a mystery. I don't ask you about your town. What's it called?

YOUNG JACK: Toledo. Toledo, Ohio.

SYLVIA: I don't ask you about Toledo, Ohio, and you don't ask me about Fotheringham Hall.

121

YOUNG JACK: Is that the name of your house? Do you really live in a house that has its own name?

SYLVIA: Oh dear, I've said too much. Do you hear that noise? That's the sheep. Someone is trying to steal the sheep. I have to go.

Sylvia exits

YOUNG JACK: Fotheringham Hall.

CROSS FADE TO LIGHTS ON TABLE.

Jack and Vera seated at table

VERA: Fotheringham Hall. She was a Land Girl, that's all she was. Miss BoPeep didn't come from a manor house. She just that to impress you. Fotheringham Hall! I'll bet you a pound to a penny that there's no such place.

JACK: Then you'd be wrong.

VERA: You mean you found it?

JACK: Yes, I found it.

VERA: Oh.

Silence. Vera rearranges the cakes, then they both speak at once

JACK: Do you miss...

VERA: Where do ...

JACK: I'm sorry, what were you going to say?

VERA: Nothing

JACK: Oh ... *Pause ..* I was just going to ask you. Do you miss it?

VERA: Miss what?

JACK: England

VERA: There are times. Sometimes in the mornings, when there's a light mist and I can smell the sea, I could almost be there. Not the way I am now, of course, the way I was then .. but it doesn't last. Really, I was glad to leave.

CROSSFADE TO LIGHTS UP CENTER

Young Vera with a baby in her arms. We hear boat whistles and crowd noises. She has just arrived in the United States.

YOUNG VERA: *(to baby)* Well where is he? Your Daddy's here somewhere. Oh dear, there are so many people. I can't see him anywhere. Now, now, don't cry. Don't worry. He knows we're coming. The army told him we'd arrive. He'll be here.

Enter Nick. He is not in uniform and he is wearing glasses. He looks around, not seeing Vera.

NICK: Well, she's not here anywhere. Perhaps she's not coming. I can always hope.

Nick and Vera see each other, but recognition is slow in coming.

YOUNG VERA: Nick, Nick, is that you? You look so different.

NICK: Yeah well, so do you. Sort of older.

YOUNG VERA: Well thanks very much. I've been through a lot you know. Things haven't been easy.

NICK: Come on, we might as well get going.

YOUNG VERA: You haven't even looked at the baby.

NICK: Yeah, cute kid.

YOUNG VERA: I named him after you, Nicholas Junior.

NICK: Good.

VERA: You don't seem very thrilled.

NICK: Hey, I don't even know if he's really mine, do I? Come on, let's get going.

YOUNG VERA: Now just a minute. What do you mean, you don't know if he's really yours?

NICK: Oh, come on Chick. Your were pretty easy weren't you? If it was so easy for me, don't you think it was just as easy for other guys. He looks a lot like Chuck to me. Yeah, see, look at that red hair.

YOUNG VERA: If you thought that, why did you marry me?

123

NICK: Because of your mother and my C.O. One thing I know for sure, the next baby is definitely going to be mine. I'm not letting you run around here the way you did in England. No Sir, you're staying home and taking care of the house. You can help my mother out. She needs another pair of hands in the kitchen. Where's your luggage?

YOUNG VERA: Over there. How long will it take to get to California? It's a long way isn't it. Are we driving or are we going by train?

NICK: Are we driving or are we going by train? Give me strength. We ain't going to California baby. You lied to me, I lied to you. That's the way it goes. don't live in California. I live right here in good old New York City.

YOUNG VERA: Oh... well ... that's alright. I'm sure New York is exciting too. The theatres, the shops ...

NICK: It ain't exactly theatres and shops in Brooklyn, babe. It's more beer joints and pawn shops.

YOUNG VERA: But you told me ...

NICK: And you told me... We both told each a lot of things, didn't we? Oh don't worry doll, we'll be okay. My mother fixed up a room for us in the attic and she's looking forward to seeing the baby. She don't know it's probably not even her grandson. My mother loves babies. Don't know what she'll make of you. I don't remember you being so scrawny looking.

YOUNG VERA: But you told me about the servants, the swimming pool.

NICK: We all had a line, baby, that was mine. Come on let's get going.

YOUNG VERA: I didn't come here to live in an attic.

NICK: Then go back where you came from.

YOUNG VERA: I can't do that.

NICK: That's right, doll, you can't do that.

CROSSFADE TO LIGHTS UP ON YOUNG JACK

Jack is studying a map and searching the horizon

YOUNG JACK: Okay, this must be it. Fotheringham Hall. Pretty impressive place. So Jack, do you just march up to the front door and ask to see Dad? That's quite some front door. I suppose there'll be a butler or footman or something ... Oh, who do I think I am? What have I got to offer a girl like Sylvia? How can I compete with all this?

Jack turns away. Enter Sylvia, dressed as a maid and carrying a basket of laundry. Jack turns and sees her.

YOUNG JACK: Sylvia

SYLVIA: *(dropping the basket)* Oh, Jack. Oh. Oh.

YOUNG JACK: Here, let me help you.

SYLVIA: You startled me. What are you doing here?

YOUNG JACK: I came to call on your father. I came to ask for your hand in marriage.

SYLVIA: No, no, you can't do that.

YOUNG JACK: It's okay darling. Trust me. I've got a speech all prepared. I'll tell him we love each other and that it's only your sense of duty to him that is keeping you from coming with me. I'll tell him that I don't plan to take you away. I'll find a way to stay here, in England, with you, I'll work alongside you and ...

SYLVIA: Oh, Jack, that sounds wonderful but ...

YOUNG JACK: Do you think he'll go for it?

SYLVIA: You don't understand.

(They finish folding the laundry)

YOUNG JACK: There, that's all of it. Your family certainly has a lot of washing.|

Sylvia stands up and Jack notices her dress and cap

YOUNG JACK: That's cute. You dress up like a maid to do the laundry.

SYLVIA: Well... I do it for ... Mummy's sake. The war, the shock, the air raids, they've sort of driven her out of her mind .. she's in somewhat of a mental ... fog and er .. . she doesn't realize that we don't have any servants any more. So when I work around the house, I dress up in the maid's clothes. That way she thinks we still have servants and she doesn't realize it's me doing all the work. After all, she didn't bring me up to do this sort of thing.

YOUNG JACK: That's wonderful of you darling.

SYLVIA: Yes, isn't it. I must go now.

YOUNG JACK: Not until I've seen your father.

SYLVIA: He's not here. He went to London.

YOUNG JACK: To London. Isn't that rather dangerous. Shouldn't he stay in the country?

SYLVIA: He went to see ... Winston Churchill.

YOUNG JACK: Churchill?

SYLVIA: Oh yes, he goes regularly. Churchill relies upon him for advice, and of course, it's no use talking to Mummy. She doesn't understand anything. You'd better go. We don't want any of the tenants to see us together.

YOUNG JACK: Sylvia, I'm not going to be here much longer. I shouldn't tell you this, but I'm being sent over to France, and I might not get back to England.

SYLVIA: Oh, Jack ... be careful. Don't get hurt.

YOUNG JACK: I'll try not to. Could I meet you later tonight?

SYLVIA: I'll come to the dance hall. We'll dance one more dance before you go.

YOUNG JACK: Tonight.

SYLVIA: Tonight.

Sylvia and young Jack freeze. Old Vera and Old Jack enter the light.

126

OLD VERA: Caught in her own trap wasn't she. She lied to you and then she couldn't find a way out of it and so she had to let you go.

OLD JACK: You're spoiling everything. Why are you doing this to me?

CROSSFADE TO LIGHTS UP CENTER STAGE

Vera, Young Vera, and Mother enter the light. Vera is holding a letter and between them they read it aloud.

YOUNG VERA: Dear Vera: Thank you for your letter which I received last week. It does take an awfully long time for letters to get over here. This was two months old by the time I got it. You'd think with the war having been over for so long, things would be a bit better.

MOTHER: I'm sorry you're not happy over there in America, but I don't know what you think I can do about it. Quite frankly, my girl, you made your bed and you are going to have to lie on it. I never did believe all that stuff about Nick having a house with servants and a swimming pool. After all why would a rich man like that be over here serving in the army and not even an officer? You could have worked that out for yourself if you hadn't had your head in the clouds. I'm sorry Nick's mother isn't very nice to you, but I suppose I can understand her point of view. Perhaps if you tried to help her in the house you might get along better. She must be very busy with 6 other sons to feed and if her husband drinks, like you say he does, she probably doesn't have much money coming in. I don't suppose she's at all thrilled to have another two mouths to feed.

VERA: Now you know, Vera, I really would like to see you and see my grandson and see how he's grown, not to mention the other baby you've had that I've never even seen a photograph of. But it's no good you thinking about coming back here. I don't have room for you. The government still hasn't repaired all the bombed out houses and I'm still sharing with Uncle Stan and Aunt Ellen, and they certainly wouldn't have room for you and two children as well. Anyway my war widow's pension wouldn't stretch to feeding you as well. I don't know how much the boat fare is to come here, but I'm sure it's more money than you can save up, particularly if Nick is out of work most of the time.

VERA, YOUNG VERA AND MOTHER: It's not that I don't love you, dear. But I really can'thelp you, not now. You're best off where you are. With love, Mum.

CROSSFADE TO LIGHTS UP ON YOUNG JACK AND SYLVIA DANCING.

YOUNG JACK: I have to ask you one last time. Will you marry me?

SYLVIA: I can't

YOUNG JACK: Can't or won't?

SYLVIA: I can't Jack. Don't ask me anymore. Let's just make the most of what we have here and now.

YOUNG JACK: That's not good enough

SYLVIA: Why, Jack, why do you want to marry me?

YOUNG JACK: Because I love you. I love you because you're brave and beautiful. I want to take away the tragedy in your life and make you happy. I love the way you speak, the way you look, your air of nobility.

SYLVIA: Oh, Jack, you don't know me.

YOUNG JACK: Yes, I do. I know all I need to know.

SYLVIA: It's not enough. Let me be a memory Jack. A beautiful memory.

YOUNG JACK: We leave tomorrow.

SYLVIA: Tomorrow. I didn't think it would be so soon.

YOUNG JACK: I've been trying to tell you.

SYLVIA: I'll never forget you Jack. Never.

YOUNG JACK: Never.

Young Jack and Sylvia dance as old Jack and old Vera enter their light.

OLD VERA: Did you ever marry?

JACK: I tried it, but it didn't last. This was all that I wanted.

VERA: She wasn't worth wasting your time on. She was playing with you. She was creating some teenage fantasy of star-crossed lovers.

JACK: Why are you trying to spoil this? What difference does it make to you?

VERA: None. No difference at all. But we're not teenagers. You've wasted your whole life because of some five minute war-time romance with a girl who thought she was a princess.

Young Jack and Sylvia continue to dance as the light come up on Nick and Young Vera. Young Vera has a suitcase.

NICK: So, you're really leaving

YOUNG VERA: Yes, I'm really leaving. I'll arrange for you to see the children if you like.

NICK: Okay, yeah. Do that.

YOUNG VERA: Well, goodbye Nick.

NICK: Where will you go?

YOUNG VERA: Do you really care?

NICK: Sure I care. They're my kids.

YOUNG VERA: That's not what you used to say. Don't worry, I won't go far. I won't go back to England, you can be sure of that much. I don't belong there any more.

NICK: Well, you sure don't belong here.

YOUNG VERA: No, you're right, I don't. I don't really belong anywhere. I have you to thank for that. Well, look after yourself Nick.

NICK: You too.

129

YOUNG VERA: Goodbye, then.
NICK: Goodbye.
Old Jack and Old Vera enter the light and watch as Young Vera and Nick shake hands and exit.
OLD JACK: What did you do?
VERA: Whatever was necessary to make ends meet. I've always done whatever was necessary. I have two wonderful children and four grandchildren and I haven't seen Nick in 20 years. Until today I hadn't even though about him. He's not something I like to think about. I've put all those memories behind me.
Od Jack crosses to Young Jack and Sylvia and takes Young Jack's place dancing with Sylvia. Young Jack exits.
OLD JACK: I'm sorry that you feel that way. My memories are my most important possession.
VERA: Then I feel sorry for you.
OLD JACK: *(stops dancing)* Sorry? There's no need to feel sorry for me.
Sylvia slips out of his arms and begins to walk away.
JACK: Where are you going? Come back.
SYLVIA: You don't need me anymore.
JACK: Yes I do. Come back.
SYLVIA: Get on with your life before it's too late.
JACK: But you are my life.
SYLVIA: No, Jack. I'm your dream. There's your life.
JACK: But I'm used to dancing with you. Come back.
Sylvia exits and Jack stand a moment irresolute. Vera watches him. Eventually Jack speaks.

JACK: *(to Vera)* Would you like to dance?
VERA: Oh, I don't know. We haven't been introduced.
JACK: If I were to introduce myself, would you dance with me?
VERA: I'll think about it.

JACK: I'm Jack
VERA: I'm Vera.

THEY DANCE TOGETHER INTO THE FINAL BLACKOUT.

FOR ALL THE SAINTS
One-Act Fantasy
First place winner Comtra Annual Theatrical Playwright's
Award
Stained glass windows spring to life in a London Basement
and an unlikely romance blossoms.
4/3M 2/3W

CAST:
Roderick the Recordkeeper
Elfrida, his wife
Marcellus the Molester (Roman Soldier)
St. Gaston de la Cordon Bleu (French Saint)
Servant to St. Gaston (non-speaking but very physical)
St. Blodwyn the Unblemished (Welsh Saint)

One set - a very cluttered underground room

SCENE: An underground room with a Gothic feel, arches or columns if possible. Entrance is down a flight of steps. One corner of the stage is designated as "Heaven", this is where messages are sent .Antique work table with a chair alongside and two benches. Piles of dusty papers on the table, plus all the props necessary to complete the action. Upstage are three large packing crates (large enough to contain a person), labels hang from the crates.

MUSIC: Open with organ music (preferably the hymn "For all the Saints")

OPENING: A woman (Elfrida) seated at the work table. She is dressed in ancient rags and tatters, so ragged that they

132

cannot be dated to any particular period of history. She is
singing to herself along with the music. Door opens and we
hear the sound of modern traffic, horns blaring, engines
running etc. When the door closes the sound is immediately
cut off.
Enter Roderick, Elfrida's husband, equally as ragged as his
wife. Roderick and Elfrida are Londoners with Cockney
accents.

RODERICK: Hello, hello, what's this then, a new delivery?

ELFRIDA: That's right, love, just arrived. I've got the papers
here on the desk. Where have you been anyway, it's long
past your tea time?

RODERICK: Got the wrong bus, didn't I? I was going down to
Fulham to have a look at some customers what might be
coming our way and I got the wrong bloody bus. I've been
everywhere, I have.

ELFRIDA: I don't know why you will go out. I haven't been up
above for at least 50 years.

RODERICK: Well, you should go out, old girl. It'll do you
good. Put some color in your cheeks.

ELFRIDA: I don't need no color in my cheeks, thank you very
much. Here. *(Handing him a sheaf of papers)* Here's the
new ones. I signed for them like usual, but you'd better
open them in case they get rough with me. I mean, look at
this one; Marcellus the Molester. Don't fancy running across
him in a dark alley.

RODERICK: *(Taking the papers).* Some of them ain't as bad as
their names. History's a funny old business if you ask me,
and church history; well, that's the strangest business of all.
Where's me tools then?

ELFRIDA: I'll get them. They're in the kitchen. I was thinking
of mending that broken chair, but then I said to myself, I said

133

"t's been broken for 75 years, 75 more won't do no harm.
Exits to kitchen
Roderick walks around, reading the labels on the large
packing cases and shouting his comments to Elfrida off-stage
RODERICK: Yeah, I see what you mean; Marcellus the
Molester, he must be a big one. I see he's from Wales; St.
Daffid in the Leeks, Pontylplriddith, Carmarthen. We ain't
had no Welsh ones for a while.(*To next case*) What's this
then? Foreign? I don't know why they're sending them here;
they must be getting full at the European depot. Who is it
anyway? (*In very badly pronounced French*) St. Gaston de la
Cordon Bleu and Servant, Chateau LaFitte, Provence. Has he
been here before?
ELFRIDA (*Off stage*): Maybe. I don't remember, but those
Frogs are always trouble.
RODERICK: I know, I know. Remember St. Joan, remember
how much trouble she was. Still afraid of matches after all
this time. *(To next case)* St. Blodwyn the Unblemished,
another Welsh one. Oh, she's from the same place as
Marcellus the Molester, I see. Well they'll be a nice pair,
won't they?
Enter Elfrida with a large claw hammer and tool box
RODERICK: Well, who shall we do first?
ELFRIDA: The Molester's been moving about in there for a
while. You'd better let him out before he gets angry.
RODERICK: Right you are then, Marcellus the Molester it is.
(*Reads delivery sheet*) Marcellus the Molester, Roman
Officer, Born AD 42, created as a stained glass window AD
1347 *(Approaches crate)* You can come out now, mate.
The crate is slashed open violently from the inside, and a man
leaps into view. He is dressed in the uniform of a Roman
soldier as he would be seen on a stained glass window. He is

134

young, very good looking. He carries an enormous sword, liberally stained with blood. Across his chest he wears a banner with the words "Marcellus the Molester , destroyer of virgins and innocents" He looks around, blinking in the light and obviously very disoriented. At first he assumes and offensive stance with his sword raised, but finally he lets the sword drop.

MARCELLUS: What the...where...who...?

RODERICK: Easy mate. Just put the sword down. *(Turning to Elfrida)* I don't like the look of that sword, do you old girl?

ELFRIDA: No, I can't say as I do. Come on now, old love. Just put the sword down.

MARCELLUS: The sword.... Oh yes, yes, I'll be glad to put it down. I feel as though I've been holding it for hours. (H*ands sword to Roderick*)

RODERICK: Hours! More like years, mate. Seven hundred to be precise.

MARCELLUS: Yes, yes... you're right of course. It's all coming back to me. *(Looking around)* Where are all the virgins and innocents? They were all around my feet last time I looked.

RODERICK: Gone, mate, gone. There's no call for that sort of stuff these days. The church ain't emphasizing martyrs no more, so they was smashed up. You were the only one they saved. (*Sets sword under table*)

MARCELLUS: What a disgusting looking thing; all that blood and gore. Of course, it wasn't like that at all you know.

ELFRIDA: No, no, I'm sure it was just an artist's impression.

MARCELLUS: Exactly so, my good woman, how very astute of you. Now, could you please tell me where I am. Obviously I am no longer in St. Daffid's in the Leeks which is a blessing in itself. Where is this exactly?

135

RODERICK: You're in London. Well, not exactly *in* London, more *beneath* London, if you take my meaning.

MARCELLUS: Londinium. So it still stands. How wonderful. How very wonderful. And who is ruler here now? Apparently not Rome - you don't look like Romans.

RODERICK: Well it's. .. Oh, I wouldn't worry about it if I were you. I've been doing this job for years, you know, unpacking you people and getting you ready for your next assignment, and I usually find that giving you a history lesson to make up for all the years you've missed is a bit of a waste of time.

MARCELLUS: Tell me at least, what year is this?

ELFRIDA: Let me see, I think it's 2013, or maybe 2014, or 15, I lose track myself. Now, why don't you let me make you a nice cup of tea? It'll settle your nerves.

MARCELLUS: Tea?

ELFRIDA: It's a relatively new invention, imported from India, but you'll like it; everyone does. I'll go and put the kettle on. Won't be long.

Exit Elfrida.

MARCELLUS: I need more explanation. Where am I and what is happening to me, and who are you?

RODERICK: Roderick the Recordkeeper at your service, sir. You see what's happened here is that you're one of the special people. Someone, 700 years ago, decided to make you into a stained glass window.

MARCELLUS: I know, I know. There I was in peaceful limbo, dead for thirteen centuries, and suddenly I am snatched back and made the centerpiece of some garish art work which depicts me slaying children and young women. My goodness man, I've been knee deep in dead and dying bodies for almost ....let me see... almost 700 years, and look what they wrote on me " Marcellus the Molester". It's not right you know. I didn't deserve that.

RODERICK: Of course you didn't mate, of course you didn't. I expect you was as white and pure as the driven snow. Look, if you don't mind, I'll just get these other crates unpacked while I talk to you. They sound like they're beginning to come around.

He continues to talk as he opens the next crate.

RODERICK: Anyhow, to cut a long story short, and it is a very long story, believe me. When you're in a window what's been dedicated like yours has, and then that window ain't wanted in the building no more, you get sent here for storage.

MARCELLUS: Storage, what do you mean storage?

RODERICK: It's a bit like limbo all over again, only you get to talk to other people. See, while you're here you can get out and walk around, eat, drink, make merry, get a bit of the other, if there's anyone willing, ... if you know what I mean... until you're sent on to another building to be used again... Ah, that's got it. Out you come.

He has opened another crate, and two figures emerge. One is a man, he can be tall and thin, or short and fat, but he should be physically unusual. He is dressed entirely in red and is wearing a golden halo. He carries a wooden spoon which he waves for emphasis when he speaks. He is meant to be an abstract stained glass representation of St. Gaston de le Cordon Bleu, a patron saint of French cooking. He speaks in heavily accented French and his manner is very theatrical. Accompanying him is a small person dressed in blue. This character is best played inside a sack of stretchy blue cloth so that he/she can appear to change shape. The character has eyes, but no mouth. This is St. Gaston's servant. He does not speak but from within the blue sack he makes his feeling known by mime. He is trembling and hanging onto St. Gaston's leg.

GASTON: Sacre blue, qu'est ce que nous avons ici?

RODERICK: (in bad French)   Hey, hey, parlez vous Anglais, s'il vous plait.

At the sound of Roderick's voice, the servant grovels in terror.

GASTON: Ah, zoot, will you leave alone my leg, you wretched creature. Go, go, scoot.

Servant crawls away a short distance. Gaston eyes Roderick and Marcellus and fixes upon Marcellus as being the person of influence. He offers a deep, theatrical bow.

GASTON: St. Gaston de la Cordon Bleu, a votre service, Monsieur.

MARCELLUS: Marcellus Maximus, Roman Governor of Pontylplriddith, and I suppose I should add; destroyer of virgins and innocents.

Reaction from Servant who has been creeping closer, but who now backs away.

GASTON: But of course, why should one wish to keep zat a secret? (*To servant*) Come back here you fool. You are of no interest to this honorable gentleman. *(To Roderick)* And you, I assume are Roderick the Recordkeeper. I have met you before.

RODERICK: You have?

GASTON: But of course. *(To Marcellus)* You must understand, Monsieur le Chevalier, I am a moderne piece of work. I am contemporary art. I am not behind the times as you ancient medieval pieces of crudite. Notice my fine art work, my flowing form. And even this miserable dog, my servant, he is well formed is he not? He has a good color. He is well made. And one thing the artiste did for which I am

138

grateful eternally, he did not give him the mouth. He is at long last silent.

RODERICK: And he's sort of multi-purpose, isn't he? He could be just about anything.

GASTON: I suppose so, but he has not the intelligence. However, as I was saying, I know who you are Monsieur le Recordkeeper. As soon as they started to remove me from my frame, I knew that I would be coming here. I have been here before, you know, in a different form. Do not worry Monsieur le Molester, this is a pleasant place. Madame Elfrida, she makes a good cup of tea.

MARCELLUS: So I've heard.

RODERICK: Well, you two just keep on chatting. I have to open the other one.

GASTON: Please, allow me to lend you my pig of a servant. *(Kicks the servant)* Over there, boy, give the gentleman whatever miserable assistance you are capable of giving. *Servant takes the hammer and attempts to help Roderick open the third crate.*

GASTON: And who is it in the crate, Monsieur Roderick? Who is going to be our companion in this place?

MARCELLUS: *(Reads label)* Oh no. Not her. (*Grabs Roderick)* Leave her in there, please.

RODERICK: Leave her in there? Don't be ridiculous. Listen to her. She's moving about already.

Muffled noises from within the crate become louder during the ensuing dialogue and the servant struggles to open the crate alone while Marcellus is detaining Roderick

MARCELLUS: You must understand, sir, er, Roderick. She's from my chapel. She was moved into St. Daffidd's about 100 years after I was installed, and she's been staring at me ever since. 600 years of chilly disapproval. St. Blodwyn the

139

Unblemished, she's a holy virgin, or member of a religious sisterhood or something of that sort. She's been looking down her nose at me day in and day out. Every morning when the sun rises there she is staring at me, and there I am knee deep in slaughtered virgins and innocents. How can I possibly meet her face to face?

RODERICK: Well, you're going to have to 'cause here she comes.

The crate is flung open, knocking over the servant, and St. Blodwyn leaps into view, full of anger. She is dressed in bright green robes, she has a halo, and her hair is completely hidden by a wimple.

BLODWYN: Get back, get back. Don't you dare touch me. I'll die before I allow you to touch me. *(Seeing servant who has crept up to take a look at her)* Aaah, what's that? What is it? It's not human. Aaah.

GASTON: Allow me, Madame *(removing Servant)*

BLODWYN: Aah, aah, what are you?

GASTON: *(Dismissing her with a wave of his hand)* What a fool of a woman. What am I? What do you think I am? I am Gaston de la Cordon Bleu, late of Chateau la Fitte, Patron Saint of Chefs and Cooks. I am the creation of the great post-impressionist artiste, Rodriguez del Questadore. Look at me, look at my form, look at my shape. How can you ask what I am?

BLODWYN: A Frenchman. Oh, saints preserve us. I've heard about Frenchmen. There was a girl in Pontylplriddith who...*(catching sight of Marcellus)* ... You?

MARCELLUS*: (With a mocking bow)* Yes, Madam, I.

BLODWYN: I never thought I'd actually see you in the flesh, actually talk to you, actually... *(She turns away, embarrassed or disgusted, it is hard to know which)*

140

MARCELLUS: My sentiments exactly, Madam. We have been looking at each other for many years, have we not?

BLODWYN: Yes, very many years. Very many weary years. But where are your victims? Where are all those poor innocents? How have you disposed of the evidence of your crimes, you.... you... Roman?

MARCELLUS: If I were to tell you that they were not my crimes, you would not believe me. However, as you can see, they have not followed me here into this place, whatever this place is.

BLODWYN: And your sword, that horrible great bloodstained sword?

MARCELLUS: Oh, that; I still have. It's around somewhere.

ELFRIDA *(entering with tea):* Oh, I see you're all up and about. I'll go back and get more cups. (*She curtsies to Gaston*) Oh, now I remember you St. Gaston, nice to see you again. Oh, look at that poor servant of yours. What did they do to the boy? *(Servant crawls up to her, making a play for sympathy. Elfrida searches in vain for his mouth).* They didn't give you a mouth did they? Well, never mind love, you come out into the kitchen with me, and we'll see what we can do. Maybe I could cut you one with a pair of scissors.

GASTON: *(grabbing servant so that a tug of war ensues)* Scissors, sacre blue, quell sacrilege. Leave him alone my good woman.

ELFRIDA: He has to have a mouth.

GASTON: No, he doesn't. If the artiste had wanted him to have a mouth, he would have given him a mouth. Who are you to dare to alter the concept of so great an artiste? You are getting ideas above your station, Madam.

ELFRIDA: Ideas above my station. Let me tell you, I'll still be here, I'll still be doing this job when you've been melted down into nothing but a paperweight, you..., you...

RODERICK: Now then, now then. Let's not have any arguing.

BLODWYN: Will someone please tell me where I am and what is happening.

MARCELLUS: From what I can make out, we are all in some sort of way station for stained glass saints.

BLODWYN: Saints? You are no saint.

MARCELLUS: Very well then, stained glass personalities. It seems *Saint* Blodwyn, that our cozy little chapel in Pontylplriddith where we spent so many happy hours staring at each other, is being demolished and you and I have been sent here for storage until we are installed in some other building. During this time, apparently, we are allowed to converse with each other.

BLODWYN: I have no intention of conversing with you.

MARCELLUS: Roderick also assures me that we can make merry and... get a bit of the other.., if we can find anyone willing. If you know what I mean.

BLODWYN: Don't be disgusting.

ELFRIDA (*dropping a curtsey)* St Blodwyn is it?

BLODWYN: Quite correct. St. Blodwyn the Unblemished. I was martyred in 1127.

RODERICK: *(Indicating Marcellus)* Oh, then it wasn't him what done you in?

BLODWYN: No, it wasn't him what done me... No, he was not responsible for my death, but that is not to his credit. He was responsible for the deaths of thousands of my countrymen.

MARCELLUS: How could you possibly know that?

BLODWYN: Because your name was a byword in our village, Marcellus Maximus. As a child I was raised on the stories of how you and your men overran our countryside, of your murdering, pillaging and... and...

MARCELLUS: And what?

BLODWYN: Raping... Ravishing... having your way with women. I've heard all about it. It's because of men like you that I decided to spend my life in solitary innocence.

MARCELLUS: Is that why, or is it because no one wanted you?

GASTON: You have a point Monsieur Marcellus. I do not think she is any fun.

BLODWYN: We are not put on this earth in order to have fun. And as for that Roman, his name was a threat, a defilement. Mothers would say to their children - behave yourself or Marcellus the Molester will get you.

MARCELLUS: But I was part of the Roman occupation and that was a thousand years before you were born.

BLODWYN: Welsh people have long memories. For a thousand years your infamous deeds have been remembered by the villagers of Pontylplriddith.

MARCELLUS: And then they made me into a window, so they would never forget.

BLODWYN: Just as they made me into a window, so that I could be venerated and adored through the centuries.

MARCELLUS: Venerated and adored. Modest, aren't you? What exactly did you do to earn this veneration and adoration?

BLODWYN: My story is well enough known, I have no need to repeat it.

RODERICK: Begging your pardon, Miss, but I ain't never heard of you before, and I've heard of most people.

143

BLODWYN: Then I suggest you look it up in one of your books. There's really no excuse for such ignorance.

RODERICK (*Crossing to table and picking up a book*) Would I find you under minor saints, or major feast days?

BLODWYN: Major feast days, of course.

RODERICK: Oh yes, of course.

BLODWYN: (*to Gaston*) I have always felt the once one becomes a saint, any modesty would be merely false modesty which would, in itself, be a form of sin.

GASTON: Well spoken, Madame, well spoken. I have always thought the same thing.

RODERICK: Here it is, here it is. It's in the appendix under Lesser Known Fast Days.

MARCELLUS: Fancy that?

RODERICK: (*Reading*) Blodwyn the Unblemished; Minor Welsh Saint, possibly martyred in 1127.

BLODWYN: Possibly martyred?

RODERICK: After ten years as a Novice in the order of the Sisters of Endless Humility...

GASTON: Ten years as a novice! Sacre bleu.

MARCELLUS: I would imagine that she was having a little trouble with the endless humility.

BLODWYN: What would you know of spiritual agony, you, you...

RODERICK: Do you want me to read this or not?

MARCELLUS: Oh, do please continue.

RODERICK: On Midsummer's Eve, the holy St. Blodwyn went forth to the shrine in the woods to pray. Whilst on her knees in prayer she was attacked by a band of robbers and rapists intent not only on robbing the saint of her virtue but also of robbing the shrine of its most precious relic, a drinking cup said to have belonged to the Virgin Mary herself. St.

144

Blodwyn died in defense of her own virtue and the sacred relic, and at the moment of her death a flight of angels appeared from heaven to drive away the robbers.

GASTON: Did you have the ones with the golden swords and the diamond lances?

BLODWYN: Of course.

GASTON: And were you transported bodily into heaven?

RODERICK: There was no body left at the shrine.

MARCELLUS: I see.

RODERICK: It was later discovered that any young maid who prayed to St. Blodwyn at the shrine in the woods would find her will strengthened to resist the sins of the flesh.

MARCELLUS: So she's a real saint then?

RODERICK (*closing the book*) Looks like it mate.

BLODWYN (*to Roderick*) My good man, how long must I remain here in the company of this unspeakable Roman?

Roderick crosses to the desk, puts down the book and checks records

RODERICK: From what I can see here, love, you haven't been sold to anyone else yet, so you'll probably be here for a while. That goes for all of you. You'll probably be here for a while, so you might as well make yourselves comfortable, and try to get along with each other.

BLODWYN: Is there no one else here, another saintly woman who could be my chaperone?

MARCELLUS: You won't need a chaperone.

BLODWYN: I have nothing to say to you.

ELFRIDA: There's only me love. I ain't no saint, but I'll make sure nothing happens to you, if you don't want it to. Some of the saints who've been here before seem to want to enjoy themselves while they've got the chance, a bit of slap and tickle if you know what I mean. After all, you're like ships

145

what pass in the night here, never to meet again, and we don't tell what goes on, do we Roderick?

Elfrida exits to get more teacups.

RODERICK: I'd better get these papers out and confirm that you're all here in good condition.

During the following dialogue, Roderick is writing papers and stuffing them into little golden message pouches

GASTON: I am sure that I will be placed immediately. For you two it is more difficult. You, Monsieur Marcellus, with your antiquated clothing, your horrible bloody sword, your ridiculous muscular form, where could they use you?

RODERICK: All kind of people could use him. Excuse me a minute. *(He picks up a bell from the desk, crosses to the "heaven" corner and rings loudly.)* Hope there's someone at home up there. *(He rings the bell again and then tosses the pouches up into the air and offstage)* Now, what was I saying? Oh yes. He might go to a gym or a spa. They might use someone like him.

GASTON: A gym or a spa, well, chacun a son gout. Each to his own. I would not want to be in a gym or a spa, but you Romans were always so.. so... physical.

BLODWYN: Animals.

RODERICK: And, begging your pardon, who do you think is going to want you?

BLODWYN: I am sure that there are many churches who would be delighted to welcome a saint such as myself.

RODERICK: I wouldn't be too sure. From what I understand, even church people like to have fun nowadays.

BLODWYN: Oh, that's really appalling.

ELFRIDA *(entering)* I've made some more tea. Why don't you all come on into the kitchen *(to servant)*. You too, love. We'll think of some way of getting it down you.

146

They all begin to exit, except Blodwyn

ELFRIDA: Aren't you coming, love? A cup of tea will cheer you up.

BLODWYN: I don't need cheering up, thank you. I have the sins and woes of the world to contemplate. It is not my duty to be cheerful.

They all exit except Blodwyn. At the last moment Marcellus hesitates and turns back.

MARCELLUS: I didn't do it, you know.

BLODWYN: Didn't do what?

MARCELLUS: Kill all those people.

BLODWYN: Of course you did. Everyone knows you did.

MARCELLUS: It was all lies put out to discredit the Roman occupation. I never raped anyone, and I only ever killed in the line of duty.

BLODWYN: I don't believe you.

MARCELLUS: You mean you don't want to believe me. After all, you've been disapproving of me for centuries, why should you change your way of thinking now?

ELFRIDA *(off stage)* Cooee, Mr. Marcellus, come and have your tea.

BLODWYN: Hadn't you better go?

MARCELLUS: Oh well, I tried. *(Exits)*

Blodwyn paces angrily, alone on the stage. A bell rings off-stage and a message pouch from the "heaven" corner lands at her feet. After making sure that she is not being watched, Blodwyn open the pouch and takes out the message. She reads it and is visibly agitated. She takes the paper and stuffs it down the front of her habit. Servant enters in time to see what she is doing.

BLODWYN: What the... oh, it's you. You didn't take long drinking your tea, did you?

Servant makes motions to indicate his lack of a mouth.
BLODWYN: Oh, I see, no way to drink the stuff. Oh well, that's your problem, not mine. Come now, don't look at me like that. Don't expect me to be sorry for you. I have worries of my own. Oh, God in heaven, you remind me of a spaniel I used to have when I was a little girl. The stupid animal was always looking at me with that hang-dog expression. Go on, get away from me.
Enter Elfrida with tea cup
ELFRIDA: Here you are dear. I brought you a nice cup of tea. I don't suppose you want to be out in the kitchen with all those rough people, you being unblemished and all. *(Pause)* You know I've met a lot of saints in my time. You wouldn't believe the people who've passed through here, but there's something about you. It's your halo, I think; it doesn't quite seem to fit. Does it feel uncomfortable, dear?
BLODWYN: No, no. I don't know what you're talking about. *(Elfrida attempts to adjust the halo)*. Take your hands off me. Leave me alone.
ELFRIDA: I was only trying to make you more comfortable. It looks like it's hurting you.
BLODWYN: It's doing nothing of the sort. I am very comfortable with this halo. Are you implying that I shouldn't be wearing it?
ELFRIDA: I'm not implying nothing, but if you ask me it looks like it was made for someone else.
BLODWYN: Someone else? Someone else! How dare you. Get out of here.
ELFRIDA: Temper, temper dear. You'd better get yourself under control. You and I may have to put up with each other for a very long time.
BLODWYN: (*clutching the front of her dress where she has*

148

hidden the message) What do you mean? What do you know?

ELFRIDA: Know? I don't know nothing. Just a feeling dear, just a feeling. *(Turns to Servant)*   Come one, love, we're going to do something about feeding you. Maybe I could make a little tiny hole and poke a straw through it. How would that be? *(Servant displays enthusiasm)* That's the spirit love. Never say die. Let's go into the kitchen and leave St. Blodwyn alone. She doesn't seem to be in the mood for company.

Exit Elfrida and servant.

BLODWYN: *(Adjusting halo).* Doesn't fit. Doesn't fit. What could she know? Of course it fits.

(She is still tugging at the halo when Marcellus and St. Gaston enter together.)

GASTON: So, I said to him, I said, I cannot permit you to do that to my souffle. My souffle is the work of art, the triumph of the human spirit, a culinary confection which flies in the face of the laws of nature. If you insist upon doing that to my souffle, I shall have to protect it with my body. And that, of course, is when he killed me and I became a martyr. Better death and burial, I said to myself, than bad cuisine and heartburn.

MARCELLUS: Of course you're quite right. As you know, we Romans were known for our love of good food.

BLODWYN: You were pigs.

MARCELLUS: Pigs?

GASTON: The lady has the point, I am thinking, Marcellus. You all ate like pigs. I hear that at your orgies, it was quite the thing to eat and eat until you were totally incapacitated, and then to take a feather and tickle...

BLODWYN: Really, must you?

149

GASTON: I was only saying......

BLODWYN: I know what you were only saying and it is perfectly revolting. Please remember to whom you are speaking.

GASTON: And you, Madame, should remember to whom you are speaking. We are seulement one saint speaking to another saint. We meet as equals.

BLODWYN: You are right, of course. One saint to another.

MARCELLUS: I never did.

GASTON: Did what?

MARCELLUS: What you said; tickled my throat with a feather, and what is more, neither did any of my comrades.

BLODWYN: You were all pigs.

MARCELLUS: You never knew us.

BLODWYN : I knew of you.

MARCELLUS: (*angrily approaching Blodwyn*) Well, I knew your people. You Welsh were a punishment visited on us by the Gods. Wild, hairy, primitive people always seeing visions, casting spells and singing all the damned time. To be stationed in Wales was worse than being stationed in hell.

BLODWYN: (*pushing Gaston aside and confronting Marcellus face to face*) Hell! That is where you should have been stationed.

MARCELLUS: (*grabbing her shoulders*) I would have preferred it. I never had one happy day in your benighted country.

BLODWYN: You knew nothing about us. I wouldn't dream of casting spells and I'm certainly not wild and hairy.

MARCELLUS: You could be for all I know. Your hair's completely covered by that veil thing. *(Long meaningful pause)* ... I've spent a lot of time wondering what color your hair is.

BLODWYN: Then you must have had very little to think about.

MARCELLUS: Very little. *(They stare into each other's eyes until interrupted by Gaston)*

GASTON: Madam, please allow me to adjust your halo. It is slipping, I think.

BLODWYN: Leave it alone. Leave me alone. All of you.

MARCELLUS: It will be our pleasure.

Enter Roderick who checks the papers on the table as the dialogue continues .

GASTON: You know, Monsieur Marcellus, it seems possible that some of us will be relocated in the New World.

MARCELLUS: New world?

GASTON: Oui, oui, the Americas. I hear it is the place to be, the place of the future. Last time I was on leave, resting one might say, as I am now, I spoke with the Senior Recordkeeper and asked if it was possible for me to be sent there. I had heard so many marvellous things, about the great cities, the music, the art, the gastronomie. But that was many years ago and instead I was sent to the Chateau Lafitte which did me great honor.

MARCELLUS: You mean we can choose where we will go - choose where we want to be and who we want to be with ? *(Glances at Blodwyn)*.

RODERICK: No, of course you can't. Gaston is just pulling your leg. Cor, can you imagine the chaos there'd be if you were all allowed to choose where you were going You wouldn't believe how many saints won't speak to each other, they wouldn't even want to be in the same church, and then of course there are a few who are just too interested in each other. Cor, it would be a nightmare sorting it all out. No, mate, you have to go where you're sent. Look, I'm overdue

for a message from Headquarters. Has anyone seen a
message come through?

BLODWYN: Message. No. Why should we have seen a
message? What sort of a message?

RODERICK: Calm down, calm down. You do get all het up
don't you? I had been making some inquiries and I was
hoping for an answer, that's all. I hate to think of you all
hanging about here for centuries, although Elfrida does like
the company.

BLODWYN: Has anyone ever done that?

RODERICK: Done what?

BLODWYN: Stayed here for centuries?

RODERICK: There have been one or two.

BLODWYN: But they found places eventually.

RODERICK: No - you know you ought to fix that halo.

BLODWYN: To hell with my halo.

GASTON: Sacre bleu.

BLODWYN: What do you mean, they didn't find places.
What happened to them?

RODERICK: Well, eventually I had to get permission to smash
them up and release them.

MARCELLUS: You can do that, smash the glass and release
the person?

RODERICK: Well, only under exceptional circumstances. It's
very rarely that it's allowed and can take as long as 200 years
to go through official channels. You needn't worry though
Marcellus old son. I know we'll find a place for you, and
Gaston should be okay - he'll fit in just about anywhere
'cause he don't really look like nothing at all. But I don't
know about you miss, somehow you don't seem to fit in.
*At that moment a message pouch lands on the stage. Elfrida
comes in from the kitchen with the Servant, and they all*

crowd around as Roderick opens the pouch.

GASTON: Alors, come along, what does it say?

MARCELLUS: Get on with it.

Roderick retrieves his glasses from a fold in his clothing, and laboriously unfolds the paper.

GASTON: Come on, come on, vite, vite, I must know my fate.

BLODWYN: Oh, what difference does it make? I don't care one way or another.

RODERICK (*reading*) Know all men by these presents, ... etc. ... etc.... They do go on don't they? Further to our earlier communication. (*He pauses and looks around*). We are happy to announce the following assignments ... St. Gaston de la Cordon Bleu - Carducci's Pizza Palace, Chicago, Grand Entrance Rotunda.

GASTON: Where is this place, this Chicago?

RODERICK: It's in America.

GASTON: Merveilleux, merveilleux, the New world. I told you Monsieur Marcellus, I told you.

He shakes hands all around.

RODERICK: Servant to St. Gaston - Carducci's Pizza Palace, Chicago, Mens Room.

GASTON (*laughing*) Aha, le pissoir.

Reaction from Servant

ELFRIDA: I am sorry, love, but orders is orders.

GASTON: Well, I at least will not have to look at him.

RODERICK: Marcellus the Molester, the Purple Lotus Health Spa, New York.

GASTON: Aha, New York, she is in the New World.

BLODWYN: Congratulations

MARCELLUS (*surprised*) Thank you.

RODERICK: Elfrida old girl, you'll have to get some more

straw. These fellows are going to need careful crating if they're going by sea.

ELFRIDA: Don't worry, I'll take care of it.

MARCELLUS: What about St. Blodwyn?

BLODWYN: It doesn't matter about me.

MARCELLUS: Of course it does - Perhaps you'll go to the New World

BLODWYN: I don't suppose I'd like it. I'd rather go back to St. Daffids.

RODERICK: They don't mention you at all Miss. No one seems to want you just now. Like I said, there's something about you that just isn't right.

BLODWYN: It doesn't matter. I really don't want to go.

GASTON: Madame Elfrida, perhaps you have some champagne set aside for occasions such as this one. I think we should all drink a toast to my fortunes and those of M. Marcellus. Come, we will go to your kitchen. *(Kicks the Servant)*. Men's room. Ah, very droll, very droll.

All exit to Kitchen except for Marcellus and Blodwyn.

BLODWYN: You had better go with them, you have something to celebrate.

MARCELLUS: I don't feel like celebrating. What's the good of being packed up in a crate and shipped across the sea and then spending the next I don't know how many years staring at the Purple Lotus Health Club, whatever that may be?

BLODWYN: It's better than being here.

MARCELLUS: I'm not sure that I agree with you. Here we can walk around, talk, eat, be people again.

BLODWYN: And here we can feel hunger, pain, envy, and all sorts of other emotions which I would prefer not to discuss.

MARCELLUS: What sort of emotions?

BLODWYN: I told you, I would prefer not to discuss it.

MARCELLUS: I'm sorry, of course, I was forgetting you are a saint and you have to resist normal human emotions. I suppose it was easy for you, just staring across that little church at me with that look of icy disapproval on your face and not feeling a damned thing.

BLODWYN: I didn't choose the expression on my face, it's the way the artist made me. Actually, people used to say that I had a very nice smile.

MARCELLUS: After several hundred years I managed to get used to your face. In fact I used to look forward to seeing it when the sun came up in the morning,

BLODWYN: You did?

MARCELLUS: I liked best on sunny spring mornings. The sun used to rise and shine right through your eyes, it lit up the whole place. I liked that very much.

BLODWYN: It used to set behind you.

MARCELLUS: Did it?

BLODWYN: Yes. There were evenings when the sunset was bright red and your whole face would glow. Of course, it made all those bleeding martyrs look much worse, but it did make your face quite handsome.

MARCELLUS: Really...

BLODWYN: Yes, really. It used to light up your hair and the muscles on your chest and legs would stand out and I used to look and ...

MARCELLUS: And?

BLODWYN: Oh nothing. Why am I saying these things?

MARCELLUS: Perhaps it's because we know we'll never see each other again and because we've waited so long for this conversation.

BLODWYN: I didn't expect you to be so...well..so...

MARCELLUS: What? So what?

155

BLODWYN: So NICE. I imagined you as a lustful, ravening beast waiting to pounce on any innocent maid who crossed your path.

MARCELLUS: Would you consider it pouncing if I.....

During this exchange they have been edging closer to each other but as Marcellus reaches out to her, Blodwyn's halo and veil slide off her head. Marcellus retreats in embarrassed horror.

MARCELLUS: Now look what I've done. I'm sorry, I really am. Here let me.....

BLODWYN (*throwing herself at Marcellus*) Don't worry about it. I never liked the damned thing.

MARCELLUS: I didn't know a Saint's halo could actually come off. I thought it was fixed permanently.

(In the next action, Blodwyn is the aggressor, forcing Marcellus back until he is prone on the bench with Blodwyn holding him down.)

BLODWYN: Then you have been misinformed - it happens all the time.

MARCELLUS: Gaston's seems quite firmly fixed.

BLODWYN: Yes, well, his would be. Look, let's not talk about my halo. Let's talk about us. You'll be leaving soon and we don't have much time.

MARCELLUS: I know. I wish it didn't have to be that way.

BLODWYN: But before you go couldn't we....

MARCELLUS: What are you suggesting?

BLODWYN: You know.

MARCELLUS: What, you and me?

BLODWYN: Yes. You and me.

MARCELLUS: But you're a saint, you're, you know... unblemished.

BLODWYN: And you're Marcellus the Molester. You could

take me. You could force yourself upon me and have your way with me.

MARCELLUS: Please, please, control yourself. I'm not going to force myself on you. *(He struggles to his feet)*

BLODWYN: Oh go on, force yourself.

MARCELLUS: I have never forced myself on anyone, not even a slave girl. I have been... well..., saving myself for the right person.

BLODWYN: What? You mean you're a ...?

MARCELLUS: Yes, that's exactly what I mean. You are not the only umblemished person here.

Suddenly Blodwyn burst into noisy tears and Marcellus whips off his banner, offering it to her to dry her eyes while making soothing noises. Meanwhile the Servant has crept into the room and is also weeping. He uses the other end of the eyes the banner to wipe his eyes and a tug of war ensues.

BLODWYN: Hey, give that to me. I'm the one who's weeping.

Servant releases the banner and looks pathetic.

BLODWYN: I'm sorry, I'm sorry. You're crying too aren't you. I don't suppose you have much to look forward to, you poor little thing. I'm sorry about what I said to you earlier. It's just that I had rather a shock and I didn't mean what I said about that dog. Actually I loved that dog, I really did.

Servant picks up the halo and offers it to her.

BLODWYN: No, no, I don't want it. I don't deserve it. Give it to him.

MARCELLUS: Of course you deserve it. I'm sure you're really a very nice person. As for your strange behavior, throwing yourself at me that way, perhaps it's just the shock of finding yourself here. I'm sure that if you were to rest quietly for a moment, you'd be back to your old self.

BLODWYN: This is my old self. You don't understand, do

157

you? Good heavens Marcellus, I've been looking at you for hundreds of years; staring right across that church at you morning, noon and night and the thoughts that have been going through my mind....I want to run my fingers through your hair and...and...(*She throws herself at him again*).

MARCELLUS: Why don't you put your halo back on? It will help you to control yourself.

BLODWYN: I can't put it back on.

MARCELLUS: Yes, you can. We can do something to make it fit.

BLODWYN: You don't understand. It won't fit ever again. It's been taken away from me. Look, look. *(She starts to rip open the front of her dress and Marcellus turns away)*

MARCELLUS: No, please control yourself.

BLODWYN: I wanted to show you this.

She hands him the crumpled note. Marcellus reads it while the servant pulls at his tunic and tries to see.

MARCELLUS: I see

Servant expresses disgust because he can't see.

MARCELLUS: There's been a mistake

BLODWYN: No. No mistake

Servant hops up and down in frustration. Blodwyn sits down next to him.

BLODWYN: You can't read, can you?

Servant shakes his head "no"

BLODWYN: Well, little one, this note is to say that St. Blodwyn the Unblemished has had her name removed from the Calendar of Saints. According to the Mother Church, I am not a saint, not now and not ever, and that's why my halo won't stay on and that's why I'm going to stay in this hole in the ground for ever and ever - Amen.

MARCELLUS: Someone might still want you.

BLODWYN: What good is a saint who isn't a saint? Look at you, they want you because you're. ..well... handsome and. ..er... sexually attractive. They want Gaston because he'll fit in anywhere, but who would want me in this ugly dress and this prune face?

MARCELLUS: You're not doing yourself justice.

BLODWYN: Oh yes, I am. Justice is exactly what I'm doing, but it's been 700 years in coming. They're quite right of course. I'm not a saint. I should never have been on the calendar. St. Blodwyn the Unblemished, what a joke.

MARCELLUS: Please, please, don't do this to yourself.

BLODWYN: Someone should have done it to me a long time ago.

MARCELLUS: But the story in the book.

BLODWYN: Oh, that!

MARCELLUS: The robbers, the rapists, the flight of angels.

BLODWYN: A pack of lies. I'm amazed that anyone ever believed it. Oh, it's true that I was a novice in the order. I had been there since I was sixteen, 10 weary years. And yes, you were quite right. Humility was my problem.

MARCELLUS: I see.

BLODWYN: You don't see the half of it. I would lie in my cold hard bed at night and wonder about what I was missing ... children, a home, a husband. Someone to love me. All I had ever really known was the convent. I became obsessed with the idea that somewhere out there in the wide world there was a man for me, a knight in shining armor, a grand passion. Eventually I knew I had to leave. That's what I was doing that night. I had made all my arrangements and I was determined to make my way to Bristol.

MARCELLUS: Why Bristol?

BLODWYN: It was the only city I had ever visited. I know you

159

think me naïve. You're right, I was naive but I had been dreaming for so long of this great lover, and I was sure he was out there somewhere waiting for me. I left the convent that wonderful moonlit night, saying that I was going to the shrine, and I met Gwendolyn from the kitchen, in the woods. She gave me clothes, I gave her my gold crucifix and I told her to tell no one where I had gone. However, it seems that Gwendolyn had a fertile imagination, and an accomplice who was eager to steal the holy relic from the shrine. The rest of the story, how I became a saint, is the result of their imagination. There were no robbers or rapists, there was no flight of angels. I simply set out on the road to Bristol, and left behind me a legend.

MARCELLUS: And what happened to you then?

BLODWYN: What do you mean?

MARCELLUS: Did you find your knight in shining armor?

BLODWYN: Not until now. *(She touches his hand briefly)*. No, Marcellus, I never reached Bristol. I died under a hedge beside the road, of cold and starvation. It turned out that there was no value to the stones in my rosary. I had no idea how to feed myself or shelter myself. I was weak and helpless and I died alone in a ditch, where my bones were never discovered.

There is a long uncomfortable silence. Blodwyn and Marcellus look at each other...look away again ....look again.

TOGETHER

Marcellus	I don't want to go to New York
Blodwyn:	The thought of staying here alone
Marcellus:	If only there was some other way
Blodwyn:	If we could be together.....

BLODWYN: Marcellus, would you do something for me before you leave?

MARCELLUS: Anything

BLODWYN: Roderick the Recordkeeper says that in special circumstances he can get permission to break up a window and release the spirit. He says that it sometimes takes as long as 200 years. I don't want to wait 200 years, please, Marcellus, take something, anything and do it for me now.

MARCELLUS: Do what?

BLODWYN: Take a hammer, an iron bar, anything, and hit me hard. Do it, please. Let me go.

MARCELLUS: He said that, he really said that?

BLODWYN: He said it would release my spirit.

MARCELLUS: Then it would release mine too wouldn't it? Blodwyn, I don't want to go to New York. I don't want to go on. I want to go with you wherever you're going.

BLODWYN: You do, you really do?

MARCELLUS: Yes, I do.

During this entire conversation, the servant is listening intently

BLODWYN: We have to find something. Something really heavy.

They search among Roderick's tools finding and discarding various unsuitable and puzzling tools, until at last Blodwyn has a very large hammer and Marcellus has an iron bar. The servant has secretly picked up one of the discarded items.

MARCELLUS: If we stand facing each other like this, I will count to three, and on the count of three we...

Enter St. Gaston, Roderick and Elfrida. Gaston is singing loudly in French with Roderick and Elfrida humming along. They are bringing bottles and glasses for Marcellus and Blodwyn. Marcellus and Blodwyn guiltily hid the instruments

161

behind their backs.

GASTON: *(To servant)* What have you there, you little pestilence? Stay out of this gentleman's belongings. Ah sacre bleu how glad I shall be when you are safely installed in this..er... pissoir. Ah what is this that has been dropped?

He picks up the crumpled note.

BLODWYN: Nothing, it is nothing

RODERICK: It looks like a communication from headquarters. Excuse me your ladyship

Pushes past and takes the note which he reads quickly

RODERICK: I see, I see. Now this does it, doesn't it? This really puts the cat among the pigeons.

ELFRIDA: What is it, love?

RODERICK: The lady here, it seems she's not really a saint, not a saint at all. She's been taken right off the bloomin' calendar.

GASTON: I knew it, I knew it. It was the halo. A true halo cannot slip that way. Ah, if there is one thing I cannot tolerate, it is an imposter.

ELFRIDA: What's that you've got behind your back?

RODERICK: One of my hammers. What was you planning to do with that? You weren't going to...?

ELFRIDA: I bet she was... and him, look at him. What's he got?

RODERICK: Both of you. Why, I've never heard of anything like it.

MARCELLUS: Now wait a minute.

GASTON: Hussy, harlot. We leave you alone with this honorable gentleman for two minutes and already you have seduced him.

Blodwyn reaches out to slap him.

GASTON: Ah mon dieu, that's a woman for you.

162

Roderick grabs Marcellus by the arm as Gaston hold onto Blodwyn

MARCELLUS: Now hold on.

RODERICK: (*As he speaks he is forcing Marcellus across the stage and into the crate. Gaston and Elfrida hold the wildly struggling Blodwyn*) No, you hold on. I'm responsible for you and I have to send you to New York I can see what you was planning and I'm not having any of it. All the years I've been here, I've never heard of such a thing. Here, Gaston, your Saintship, help me crate him up.

MARCELLUS: What? What on earth...

Marcellus struggles fiercely but eventually Roderick and Gaston force him back into his crate while Elfrida holds onto Blodwyn

BLODWYN: Let me go, let me go.

ELFRIDA: Oh, just keep still ducks. It ain't no good you struggling like that. Rules is rules.

RODERICK: Right, now you stay there till they come for you... there'll be no more of this nonsense. *He grabs hold of Blodwyn and begins to tie her up.* As for you Miss Blodwyn, you're going to be tied down.

BLODWYN: You can't make me stay here, please, please.

RODERICK: I have to go through channels. Maybe eventually I'll get permission, but until then you stay here.

Blodwyn is tied to a chair. When the job is finished, Roderick, Elfrida and Gaston are out of breath.

ELFRIDA: She's a strong one and no mistake.

She drinks a glass of wine to revitalize herself and passes the bottle around to the other two.

BLODWYN: Marcellus, Marcellus, can you hear me?

ELFRIDA: Not in there, he can't.

BLODWYN: Please, please. I want him to know that I love him.

GASTON: And whyfor should he be interested in knowing that?

BLODWYN: You, you.....

GASTON: Watch your tongue.

RODERICK: St. Gaston, you keep a sharp eye on her while I go upstairs. We used to have a cage up there, didn't we, Elfrida?

ELFRIDA: You mean the one that came with the window of Daniel in the Lion's Den?

RODERICK: That's the one.

ELFRIDA: It's in the attic, but it will need cleaning out. Remember when we had St. Francis of Assisi and all those birds and squirrels....

RODERICK: How can I forget? What a mess that was. That was a right old how's yer father, that was. Well, go on old girl, go and get your scrub bucket.

GASTON: Never fear, I will her carefully watch.

Exit Roderick and Elfrida

Gaston circles Blodwyn teasingly. While he is doing so, the Servant creeps to the corner and finds a length of rope, and as Gaston is circling Blodwyn, the Servant is circling behind him. Blodwyn, seeing what is happening, tries to keep Gaston's attention.

GASTON: So what was it you planned to do? You planned to escape, huh? To shuffle off this mortal coil? And where did you think you would go, you saint who is not a saint?

BLODWYN: Into the light.

GASTON: Into the light? What does this mean?

BLODWYN: There is a place, I know there is. There was a night once a long time ago when I was almost there.

GASTON: I don't know what you are talking about.

BLODWYN: *(Desperate to keep his attention)* A moonlit night, a moonlit midsummer night in the mountains. I was looking up at the stars....

GASTON: What nonsense you women talk.

BLODWYN: No, no, it's not nonsense. It's the truth. I was looking up at the stars and thinking about love, real, true love.

GASTON: Sacre bleu, I don't want to hear any more of this.

BLODWYN: You don't know about love, do you? All you know about is food.

GASTON: Food, love, they are the same thing. They...

The servant trips him with the rope and wrestles him to the ground.

GASTON: Sacre bleu, mon dieu, qu'est ce que c'est..... Leave me alone. How dare you....

BLODWYN: Careful, careful, don't smash him whatever you do. I don't want him coming with me. Oh hurry, hurry, they'll be back.

At last the Servant has Gaston tied down and is able to release Blodwyn. Together they search for something to open Marcellus' crate.

BLODWYN: There has to be something. Not this, not this, this will never do. What about this?

Desperately she wrenches open the crate and Marcellus steps out into her arms. He tries to kiss her but she pulls away.

BLODWYN: Not now, not now. Perhaps there'll be a time and a place later. Quickly, take this (*hands him crowbar*) We have to do it now before they come back. Where's the hammer?

She finds the hammer and they stand facing each other. Servant stands away by the tool box. At the last moment Blodwyn turns and runs to hug him.

BLODWYN: Thank you, thank you. I am eternally grateful.

Again she and Marcellus stand face to face.

MARCELLUS: On the count of three.

BLODWYN: On the count of three.

Servant picks up a hammer and prepares, unnoticed by the others to strike himself on the head.

Roderick bursts onto the stage

RODERICK: What the blazes are you doing?

MARCELLUS: One, two three..........

Brief blackout, all exit. Various lighting effects and then a pale gold center stage spot into which walk Marcellus and Blodwyn while a heavenly chorus sings a hymn (preferably For all the Saints)

"The golden evening brightens in the west
    Soon, soon to faithful warriors cometh rest"
   "Sweet is the peace of Paradise the blest
    Halleluia, Halleluia."

During the final chorus, servant enters the light, unties the top of his sack and emerges as a young man, or young woman. They exit together with servant in the center, into a very bright light.

CURTAIN

Printed in Great Britain
by Amazon